THIRTY DAYS
IN MAY

THIRTY DAYS
IN MAY

The Day-by-Day Drama of the 1970 Indy 500

HAL HIGDON

Octane Press, Edition 2.0, May 2022
First Edition, G. P. Putnam's Sons, New York, 1971
Copyright © 1971 by Hal Higdon

On the cover: 1970 Indy 500 starting grid from back
to front: A. J. Foyt's red number 7, Johnny Rutherford's
yellow number 18, Al Unser Sr.'s blue number 2.
Cover image created by Dalaney LaGrange

ISBN: 978-1-64234-060-0
ePub ISBN: 978-1-64234-067-9

LCCN: 2021952419

Design by Tom Heffron
Copyedited by Faith Garcia
Proofread by Brad Allard

octanepress.com

Octane Press is based in Austin, Texas

Printed in the United States of America

Indianapolis Motor Speedway has hosted many great races, and the 1970 Indy 500 may be the greatest. For that very reason, this book has been put back in print more than a half century after its original publication.

Also worthy of note is that Memorial Day used to be celebrated on May 30. So, in this book, thirty days in May was actually thirty days. Memorial Day is now positioned on a Monday, so the number of days from May 1 to the race is often less than thirty.

—Hal Higdon, November 2021

CONTENTS

Prologue

The track stood silent on the thirtieth day of April. A hot southwest wind stirred trees near the main gate. Only a handful of tourists wandered through the museum outside the grandstand, gazing at the old cars.

The following day the noise would begin. On May 1, 1970, the track would open for practice, and the scream of angry engines would carry across Georgetown Road, rattling windows in the homes of Speedway, Indiana. In thirty days, track owner Tony Hulman would announce: "Gentlemen, start your engines." The world's greatest sporting event would begin. With the shift of Memorial Day to Monday, the gap between track opening and that signatory command no longer is an exact thirty days. Tony Hulman no longer is around. But in the month of May, Indiana functions as the center of the auto racing world.

Each Memorial Day roughly 300,000 people watch the Indianapolis 500-mile auto race in person. Millions more listen on radio or watch theater telecasts. The 500 offers more money for drivers than any other auto race. In 1970, the purse would reach one million dollars.

But on April 30, the excitement had not yet begun.

"The curves are all banked nine degrees," the Speedway tour guide told a group of tourists as their tour minibus moved slowly through the first of the track's four turns. "They're sixty feet wide, a quarter of a mile in length. The long straightaways are fifty feet wide, five-eighths of a mile in length. There are two short straightaways an eighth of a mile in length."

The guide pointed to a pair of signal lights at the end of the short straightaway between Turns One and Two. "During the race when that yellow light is on," he said, "each driver has to hold his position. He can't go around anybody. And the green light, of course, is the go signal."

The bus completed Turn Four safely and rolled down the main straightaway. Grandstands lined both sides of the track. The guide turned the bus onto a strip of cement separated from the main straight-away by grass and a low wall. "This is the pit area," he said. "It's thirty-five feet wide. Over here to your left are thirty-three pits right down the line."

On the wall, the names of last year's drivers could still be seen faintly: Bobby Unser, Mel Kenyon, Mark Donohue, Dan Gurney. The guide continued: "The winner of the last race was Mario Andretti, in car number 2. His pit is to the left here. His average speed for the 500 was better than one hundred fifty-six miles per hour.

"The boy that had the pole position in the last race was A. J. Foyt. He qualified at better than one hundred seventy miles per hour. A. J. is a three-time winner. This is his pit."

The guide stopped the bus before a gap in the stands inside the track. A banner hung above the gap read: GASOLINE ALLEY. Beyond the banner was a fenced-in compound and long rows of garage doors. The guide identified Gasoline Alley as the area where the mechanics readied their cars for the race.

At that moment, a loudspeaker crackled in Gasoline Alley: "Gentle-men, the track will open for practice tomorrow morning at nine. When it does there will be a speed limit of one hundred sixty miles per hour."

The original Indianapolis 500, or more familiarly the Indy 500, was held in 1911. The first winner was Ray Harroun. He averaged a sheepish seventy-four miles per hour. Many great races have been contested on the Indianapolis Motor Speedway since then. This race is among the greatest!

The thirty days in May of 1970 are about to begin.

Getting underway

On Friday, the first day of May in 1970, a gray sky hung over the Indianapolis Motor Speedway. The track lay wet from an early morning rain.

By nine the sun appeared briefly. "Get a car out here!" shouted one mechanic. But the yellow light still flashed atop the tall scoring pylon, a signal that the track remained closed.

The mechanics stood before their garage doors, sipped hot coffee, gazed up at the sky, and waited.

Car owners had filed entries for eighty-four racing machines, but only twenty-eight had arrived in Gasoline Alley by the first day of practice. Twelve would never arrive, though their owners had each paid $1,000 in entry fees.

At the north side of the garage area, two mechanics in orange coveralls pushed an orange car toward the fuel pumps. The car's number was 79. It was one of three racers brought to Indianapolis by driver and owner Bruce McLaren of New Zealand.

One of the mechanics, Alan McCall, started to fuel the car. Unlike passenger automobiles, which use gasoline, racing cars burn methanol (also known as methyl alcohol). Methanol is a colorless liquid. It can increase the power output of an engine by 10–15 percent, although with a 50 percent decrease in mileage. Most Indianapolis race cars get roughly two miles per gallon. In the 500-mile race they must stop three times to refuel.

Alan pumped thirty gallons into the car's left tank. Then he pumped the same amount into the right tank. Finally, he and the other mechanic rocked the car back and forth and squeezed in three more gallons.

"I think that's full," said Alan, speaking with a New Zealand accent.

A man wearing a tweed coat with a USAC (United States Auto Club) armband glanced at the fuel pump. He marked 63.1 gallons on his clipboard. Alan meanwhile stuck a plastic hose into the car tank and began siphoning off fuel. He was determining the capacity of the car's fuel tanks.

The official handed Alan the clipboard. "We need your signature here," he said.

Alan leafed through the papers on the clipboard. They represented the United States Auto Club's technical inspection of the McLaren car. Before any car can practice at Indianapolis, it must earn USAC approval. The car must have a wheelbase of at least ninety-six inches and must not exceed an overall length of sixteen feet. The engine size is limited. Alan finally signed the papers and returned the clipboard to the official.

At the other end of Gasoline Alley, near the entrance to the track, a white car numbered 54 sat on a large scale. THE CITY OF MEMPHIS SPECIAL was lettered in orange and black on the machine's side. It was owned by aircraft parts dealer Jack Adams and was the only turbine car at Indianapolis—although Adams also had two Offenhauser-powered cars. The chief mechanic, Howard Millican, juggled the scale's weights. A USAC official approached. "I just checked it," Howard told him hopefully. "Looks like it's six ounces over."

The official paid no attention and juggled the weights himself. "Thirteen-fifty exactly," he announced.

USAC rules specify a minimum weight for each car of 1,350 pounds. You can be heavier, but you can't be lighter. In contrast, most American passenger cars weigh 3,500 to 4,500 pounds. A Volkswagen weighs 1,800 pounds. The cars are weighed three times: during technical inspection, after they qualify, and following the race—*if* they finish in the top ten.

On the south side of Gasoline Alley, a bright green car numbered 21 sat before a garage labeled VOLLSTEDT ENTERPRISES. The name of 21's driver was lettered on the cockpit: JOHN CANNON.

Mechanic Hal Sperb stood at the rear of the car, his hand on the throttle lever, revving the engine: *ROOM! ROOM! ROOM!* A group of race fans stood outside the fence staring in at the action. Sperb revved it again and watched the dials in the cockpit. With each scream of the engine, the tachometer needle would bounce to near 8,000 revolutions per minute.

A slender man with gray hair stood nearby, wiping his hands with a rag. "Hey, Vollstedt," one of the fans outside the fence shouted to him, "a guy bet me fifty dollars that you won't be the first one on the track." Rolla Vollstedt smiled and continued to wipe his hands on the rag. The last six out of seven years at Indianapolis he had gotten his car onto the track before anyone else.

Several doors away, the walls of a double garage had been painted with red and white vertical stripes. A red, white, and blue star-spangled car sat parked inside. It would be driven by Lloyd Ruby of Wichita Falls, Texas.

A crewman talked with a friend about being caught in a tornado while passing through Oklahoma City the day before. "Twelve automobiles in our motel parking lot had their windshields blown out," he said. "We were lucky Lloyd's car didn't get damaged."

Further down the line, Howard Millican attached a USAC sticker on his car, showing it had passed technical inspection. Millican told a reporter that this was the fifty-fourth annual Indianapolis race, and the number of their turbine car was 54. "This is probably the simplest car ever built for this track," the mechanic explained. "There are no oil coolers. We have batteries on board for self-starting. We get better mileage than the piston cars, so we can run with only thirty gallons of fuel. This is good for safety."

"Has the car run before?" asked the reporter.

"Just up the road in front of my home in Danville, Indiana," Howard replied.

Shortly afterward, they pushed the turbine car to the track. The weather had cleared. A driver with curly blond hair followed, carrying his helmet under one arm. When he arrived at the pits, one of the crewmen pointed to the name stitched to the front of his uniform: JIGGER SIROIS. "What did you say your name was?" asked the crewman.

"Oh," said the driver, and he rushed back to the garage to change uniforms. He was actually Rick Muther of Laguna Beach, California. In the excitement of opening day, Muther had grabbed the uniform of his teammate by mistake. Jigger stood nearby laughing.

Although he had yet to race a single lap at Indianapolis, Leon D. "Jigger" Sirois already had achieved fame—of a kind—at the track. As a rookie at Indianapolis in 1969, Jigger's name was drawn first for qualification attempts. A qualifying run consists of four laps. After Jigger went three laps at a slowish 161 miles per hour, his crew raised the yellow flag to cancel the attempt. Even before Jigger pulled into the pits, the rain started. It rained for two days, and nobody qualified that weekend.

The following weekend, Jigger went slightly faster, but his crew still waved him off. Thirty-three other drivers qualified for the race. Had his crew accepted his original time, not only would Jigger have made the race, but he also would have won the pole position—worth more than $20,000 in various awards.

By eleven o'clock a half dozen cars waited in the pit area near the south exit onto the track. They included the turbine, Vollstedt's car, and the Art Pollard Car Wash Special number 10. Art Pollard sat in the cockpit. Toward the center of the runway, three empty orange McLaren cars stood in a row.

The green light flashed at the end of the straightaway. The turbine engine began to wail. But the yellow light came on in place of the green. Chief steward Harlan Fengler cautioned the drivers over the loudspeaker that no engines were to be started yet. At the Speedway, Fengler's word is law. Pollard's crew waited squatting. They had a portable battery starter already fitted into their car's rear end. At 11:35 a.m. Fengler announced: "The track is now open for practice." The green light flashed.

Art Pollard's engine roared, and his crewmen pushed him toward the track. But suddenly his engine died. The crew ran to retrieve their car and driver for a restart. But the whine of the turbine rose as The City of Memphis Special moved onto the track. Rolla Vollstedt's car quickly followed, not first but a close second.

An hour later the three McLaren cars began practice runs: Denis Hulme in car number 73, Chris Amon in car 75, and Bruce McLaren himself in car 79. Nine cars tested the track on the first day in May, running under the 160-mph speed limit. Denis Hulme ran the fastest single lap of 158.8 mph, with Lloyd Ruby turning 158.4 mph. All eyes, however, focused on Team McLaren.

As the three orange cars glided single file around the two-and-a-half-mile oval, veteran race observers nodded. An old adage at Indianapolis says that the drivers ready and running the first day are the ones to beat.

The Indianapolis Motor Speedway and Museum

Tony Hulman appeared on Saturday, the second day of May, to present chief steward Harlan Fengler with the official keys to the Speedway. Hulman had bought the track from Eddie Rickenbacker in 1946. That year George Robson won the race by half a minute over Jimmy Jackson. Now, twenty-five years later, Jackson drove Robson's car around the track in an opening weekend ceremony. Rick Muther took an honor lap in the turbine car. The weather was cool.

At the corner of Sixteenth Street and Georgetown Road, a line of people stood outside the one-story Speedway Museum and office. Some wanted to buy tickets, but only a few ten-dollar seats remained. All the best seats along the main straightaway had been sold nearly a year before to the people who sit in them year after year.

The Indianapolis Speedway contains 220,000 seats, costing up to thirty-nine dollars each. Another 100,000 or so fans pay five dollars on race day for "standing room" in the infield. In terms of one-day attendance, the 500 race is the number one sporting event in the world. Broadcaster Sid Collins describes it as "the greatest spectacle in auto racing."

The rest of those in line waited to visit the racing museum, which occupies half the Speedway office building. They filed slowly through the door and past a green Cooper Climax parked in the front window. Australian Jack Brabham had driven the green car at Indianapolis in 1961.

Many racing people considered green unlucky. Old-time driver Barney Oldfield once crashed a green car. Before Brabham appeared in his green racer, few drivers dared to tempt fate by using green.

Brabham also was the first to drive a rear-engine car at Indianapolis. It was underpowered, a Formula One car from the European Grand Prix circuit. Nevertheless, Brabham finished ninth.

Four years later, British driver Jim Clark won at Indianapolis in a rear-engine car (also green) that ended the reign of the front-engine roadsters. The rear-engine cars handled better, partly because with no drive shaft under the driver they could be built lower to the ground, and partly because the weight over the rear wheels provided better traction. Only Jim Hurtubise continued to return to the Speedway with a front-engine car.

Ray Harroun won the first Indianapolis 500-mile race in 1911. Harroun's yellow Marmon Wasp is among the dozen racing machines exhibited in the Speedway Museum. It is a high, squarish automobile with a fin perched atop its pointed tail. Most race cars of that era carried two passengers: a driver and a mechanic. Harroun, however, rode alone. He mounted a mirror on the hood so he could see cars approaching from behind. It was the first rear-vision mirror installed in any automobile.

The Speedway had been built several years earlier by a group of four Indianapolis businessmen, headed by Carl G. Fisher. Fisher believed a motor speedway would turn Indianapolis into the auto capital of the world—and help promote his headlight business. The four investors purchased 320 acres of farmland five miles from downtown. Construction began in the spring of 1909 on a two-and-a-half-mile oval track. The surface was crushed stone and asphaltum oil.

On June 5, 1909, the Speedway opened. The first auto program featured races from five to three hundred miles, spread out over three days beginning Thursday, August 21.

In the feature 250-mile event, the surface of the track soon began to break up. Midway through the race, driver William Bourque glanced over his shoulder at another car approaching. In that instant his machine veered to the right, its front wheel hitting a hole. The car spun into a ditch, somersaulted, and landed upside down. Bourque and his mechanic, Harry Holcomb, died, the Speedway's first casualties.

Another driver, Fred Ellis, died of heat exhaustion while trying to restart his car by cranking it. Bob Burman eventually won the race, averaging 153.77 miles per hour. Two days later another crash cost the life of a mechanic and two spectators. Six people had died in the first weekend of Speedway racing.

Fisher decided the track needed a better surface. It took sixty-three days to lay three million bricks around the oval. A concrete guardrail was built to protect spectators.

In December 1909, only a few freezing fans appeared for speed trials. That summer a series of different automobile, airplane, and balloon races failed to attract large crowds.

Fisher finally decided to give the fans a *single* 500-mile race each year on Memorial Day. Eighty thousand people appeared in 1911 for the first 500 race and saw Ray Harroun win in the car now displayed at the Speedway Museum.

The museum also contains a collection of historical sparkplugs, engines, and other mementos—like, for instance, the first crash helmet worn by Wilbur Shaw in the 1932 race. Other drivers laughed at Shaw then and called him a sissy. Later, at another track, Shaw flipped from his crashing car, landed on his head, and survived to win three 500 races. Today no driver is considered a sissy for wearing a full-head helmet, fireproof clothing, and safety belt and harness.

Shaw's winning car from 1939 and 1940 is displayed at the museum.[1*] Among other winning cars displayed are those driven to double victories by Mauri Rose in 1947 and 1948[2†] and Bill Vukovich in 1953 and 1954.

But nowhere among the many photos in the Speedway Museum will you see one that shows what happened to Bill Vukovich when he returned the following year, seeking his third straight victory. Leading by seventeen seconds at 125 miles, he prepared to pass three trailing drivers: Rodger Ward (who later would win at Indianapolis in 1959 and 1962), Al Keller, and Johnny Boyd.

Suddenly, Ward's axle broke. He swerved out of control. Keller dodged and struck Boyd, knocking him into Vukovich's way. Vukovich

---

[1*] Shaw won in 1937 in a different machine.
[2†] Rose also won in 1940 as codriver with Floyd Davis.

hit Boyd, and his car flew over the outer wall, bounced fifteen feet in the air, bounced again, and landed upside down in flames. Vukovich died of a skull fracture.

Fifteen drivers have died in the 500 race; eighteen others have died while practicing for it. A dozen mechanics died back during the age when two rode in the cars. But fatalities go unrecorded at the Speedway Museum. Tony Hulman's museum chooses to discuss other things—checkered flags, horsepower, miles per hour—and perhaps it is best this way.

The drivers themselves dislike discussing the danger that lurks at the end of each straightaway. They understand that winners succeed by driving on the thin edge of control. Sometimes they push over that edge and crash. A certain fear among drivers is healthy; it keeps them alive.

Among the mementos of success in the Speedway Museum is the Sheraton-Thompson Special that A. J. Foyt Jr. drove to victory in 1964. Foyt also won in 1961 and 1967. In 1970, he hoped to become the track's first four-time winner.

A. J. Foyt

Sunday proved to be a quiet day at the Speedway. A rabbit darted across the track, only to be struck and killed by Joe Leonard in his Johnny Lightning Special. Leonard also had the day's fastest time, 162.279 miles per hour, breaking Harlan Fengler's 160 mph "speed limit." But many of the drivers spent the afternoon either watching or racing in the Yankee 250 at Indianapolis Raceway Park. A. J. Foyt won a full lap ahead of Roger McCluskey.

By any measuring stick, Anthony Joseph Foyt Jr. ranks as the top American race driver of all time. In addition to his three 500 victories, Foyt has won five USAC national championships, more than any previous driver. By 1970, he had scored a record forty-two victories in championship cars and had won a total of 151 major races. All but five of these victories came in the 60s. Between 1959 and 1966, A. J. drove eighty-seven consecutive championship races, a record many people think will never be equaled.

Foyt dislikes losing—as several of his mechanics discovered. When his car failed mechanically, Foyt often exploded with anger. He and his mechanic, George Bignotti, feuded continuously during six years together. The two split, then drifted together again. After an angry argument at Langhorne, Pennsylvania, in 1965, Bignotti finally quit for good.

During the next season Johnny Pouelson worked for Foyt. At Indianapolis in 1966, the crew worked two nights preparing Foyt's racer. Foyt demanded still more changes. It was early in the morning. Pouelson wanted to pause long enough to shave and eat. Foyt said no. Pouelson sold his tools and left immediately. "Working with Foyt is like working with a live volcano," comments another race mechanic.

Officials who cross A. J. Foyt also find him a difficult man. Foyt once was fined $1,000 for arguing too loudly with a race promoter. Another time a trackside fight with a driver who had cut him off almost cost Foyt a year's suspension from racing.

In a car, however, Foyt becomes the perfect professional: he never displays his anger. Foyt drives hard but fairly. "The reason I've always respected Foyt," says Mario Andretti, "is that while he's got a very quick temper off the track, I've never heard of him doing anything foolish while racing. And that's saying an awful lot for a guy with a temper like Foyt's."

Foyt also takes no guff from sponsors. In 1964, Goodyear hired him to test their tires. Foyt decided Firestone made better tires for the 500 and used *them* in the race. He did wear a Goodyear suit, however, and refused to accept prize money from Firestone. Later, he began racing on Goodyear tires, but wore a Firestone cap. In 1965, Foyt switched from Offenhauser to Ford engines, but he continued to use Champion sparkplugs instead of the Ford-made Autolites.

A. J. Foyt Jr. was born in Houston in 1935. His father was a race driver and mechanic. When A. J. Jr. was three years old, his father built him a tiny red racing car with a one-cylinder Briggs & Stratton engine. At age five, he drove between feature events at tracks around Houston. In 1946, his father owned two midget racers and took one of them to a Dallas event. When he returned later that night, Foyt Sr. found the front and back yards rutted with tire tracks. The racer sat smoldering in the garage after having caught on fire. Young A. J. lay in bed pretending to be asleep.

Foyt dropped out of school in the eleventh grade. He drove midget racers, wearing bright white trousers and silk shirts, and earned the nickname Fancypants. In 1958, he arrived at the Speedway. Foyt qualified his first three years but placed no higher than tenth.

In 1961, Foyt battled Eddie Sachs for the lead. During what should have been his last pit stop, Foyt's fueling equipment failed, and Foyt had to return for more fuel with only fifteen laps to go. This should have given the race to Sachs, but Eddie had to pit three laps from the finish to change tires. Foyt won his first 500.

Three years later, in 1964, Bobby Marshman led but lost an oil plug; Jim Clark led, but his tire split; Parnelli Jones led but caught fire during a fueling stop. A. J. Foyt assumed the lead on the fifty-fifth lap and held it to the finish.

Three more years later, in 1967, Foyt won his third 500 victory when gearbox failure halted leader Parnelli Jones three laps from the finish. In 1970, a sign on the wall of Foyt's garage said: LUCK IS WHERE PREPARATION MEETS OPPORTUNITY.

Foyt's Indianapolis victories made him a millionaire. He built an expensive house for his wife Lucy and their three children. Even so, he continued to race, even in minor events. "He will show up at an obscure dirt track, having spent more to get there than he could possibly win," wrote Lyle Kenyon Engel in *The Incredible A. J. Foyt*. "Then he will drive flat out against young drivers who have everything to gain by beating him. They seldom do. They would like to win, but Foyt *must* win. Winning is his life."

During his long racing career, A. J. Foyt seemed immune to serious injury. But during a 1965 stockcar race in Riverside, California, Foyt's brakes failed coming into a sharp turn. Rather than hit two other cars, he swerved over a thirty-foot embankment. His car rolled end-over-end, demolishing itself. A. J. broke a vertebra and a bone in his left heel. Undaunted, he qualified, four months later, for the pole in record time at Indianapolis. (He led for ten laps but failed to finish because of rear-end gear failure.)

In 1965 and 1966, Mario Andretti won the USAC national championships, but 1967 was a good year for A. J. Foyt. He won at Indianapolis. He teamed up with Dan Gurney at Le Mans, and they became the first Americans ever to win the twenty-four-hour race. Going into the final championship event of the season, Foyt held a narrow 340-point edge over Andretti in the battle for the national championships. Six hundred points would go to the winner of the 300-mile race at Riverside. If Mario won with A. J. no better than fifth, Andretti could win his third straight national title, something even Foyt had failed to accomplish.

On the fiftieth lap at Riverside, Al Miller spun and Foyt crashed into him. Foyt had entered Jim Hurtubise in a backup car, so he ran back to the pits. Hurtubise, however, had been black-flagged because of an oil leak. Foyt flagged down Roger McCluskey (who also ran on Goodyear tires) and climbed into his car. Foyt finished fifth, splitting the points awarded with McCluskey. Andretti took third but lost the national championships by eighty points to Foyt.

In 1968 at Indianapolis, rear-end problems halted A. J. at eighty-six laps. In 1969, he placed eighth after a twenty-two-minute pit stop. But in 1970, his fans noted with hope that every third year was a Foyt year. Foyt himself admitted: "If I don't win, I'll get superstitious."

No other driver had won four times at Indianapolis. But most people figured even that achievement wouldn't keep A. J. from returning for victory number five the following year.

Driving the track

"**H**ere he comes!" shouted one of two fans sitting in Grandstand E.

A blue racer moved down the straightaway, growing in size as it approached. Heat waves danced off the car's rear deck, blurring the track behind. There was little noise, only a rising hum.

Then the racer veered, turning left, ducking down into Turn One, and showing its number—a streak of blue as it darted past where the two fans sat watching.

Finally, the noise *RARRRRRGHHHHHH!* An angry rasp echoing against the upper deck over their heads, then dying as the car slid through the turn and out into the short straightaway, coming close, very close, to the wall then ducking down again through Turn Two. As the racer streaked along the back straightaway, mostly unseen because of trees in the infield, the rasp turned again into a hum.

"Forty-eight!" shouted the other fan.

"Dan Gurney," his friend identified the car.

"Here comes another!"

A second car pulled out of the pits: a red, white, and blue racer with the number 10 on its side. Art Pollard sat in the cockpit. He moved slowly along the inside lane of the track, driving to the left of the double yellow line going through the turn. Inside the line there was about five yards more of track, then another thirty yards of grass before the high wire fence that kept spectators away.

A guard in a yellow Speedway shirt stood nearby, a fire extinguisher by his side. Two observers watched from a wooden tower. Should an accident occur, they could have fire trucks, ambulances, and wreckers rolling within seconds.

The sun was out, and the day was warm, and the people came on Monday to watch the drivers practice. Gurney drove into the pits his next time around. Pollard came by a second time, still moving slowly on the inside.

The sound of a starting engine could be heard from Gasoline Alley more than a quarter mile away. Pollard approached again, but now he had moved up near the straightaway wall. As he came through the turn, he stayed above the yellow lines. "He's rolling now!" shouted one of the fans in Grandstand E.

Chief steward Harlan Fengler had lifted his 160-miles per hour speed limit that morning, and some of the drivers began reaching for race speed. As Pollard moved through the turn and up toward the wall on the short chute, he followed a dark smudge, about a half-dozen feet wide, that circled the track. He was in the "groove."

The groove was dark gray—compared to the light gray of ordinary asphalt—and it would get darker. There is a quick route around every track: Wide here. Close there. Aim for that! The better drivers know this route. As they drive lap after lap after lap, their tires lay down a thin layer of rubber. As more rubber builds up, the groove gets darker. It also offers better traction. Cars moving along it can go faster.[3]

Pollard rocked down the straightaway again and into the turn. Suddenly, the rear end of his car wiggled. The wiggle lasted but a fraction of a second, then he recovered. He flowed smoothly around the rest of the turn. Such a wiggle during a qualification run might cost a driver several miles per hour in his lap time and perhaps a place in the race. If the wiggle developed into a spin, it could cost him his car—or his life.

At the end of that lap Pollard drove into the pits. He had learned something more about his car, about the track, and about himself.

Drivers call the section of the track wide of the groove the gray stuff. When a driver running at full speed moves into this area, he's in trouble—not merely because of poorer traction, but because one doesn't

---

3 Author Hal Higdon would title another of his auto racing books *Finding The Groove*.

slide into the gray stuff unless he is out of control. When British driver Mike Spence died against the wall while practicing for the 1968 race, the track observer on the turn flashed the yellow light even before he began to spin. Spence had edged into the gray stuff. The observer knew he had lost control.

The top drivers don't need a dark line to guide them around the Speedway's two-and-a-half-mile oval. Mario Andretti, A. J. Foyt, Lloyd Ruby, Al and Bobby Unser, and Dan Gurney have driven hundreds of laps at Indianapolis, not only during the month of May but also while tire testing at other times of the year for Firestone or Goodyear. They know each foot of the track. Foyt may brake at a slightly different point than Andretti. Ruby may angle into certain turns unlike Gurney. But the basic pattern used by drivers at Indianapolis is identical.

As they come down the main straightaway, they stay up near the wall—but not too close. On the straightaway an Indianapolis race car reaches speeds of 210–215 mph. In a single second they cover the length of a football field. If the driver moves too close to the wall, the air he pushes aside will bounce back at him, buffeting his car. "It sets your goggles vibrating and pounds at your ears," claims Mario Andretti. "If you ever try to stay up there near the wall, you know right away that something's really wrong."

Just before the end of the straightaway, however, the driver moves up toward the wall for a brief instant to allow a better angle moving through the corner. (He already will have eased up, "backed off" on the throttle, and hit his brakes.) Then he turns the wheel left and dives into the corner, pinching as close to the insides as possible. In the short chute his car will drift wide. If his nose is pointed too far outward, he may hit the wall. But if he pinches too tightly, his rear end may "break loose" into a skid.

A driver guides his racer through the turn not only with the steering wheel, but also with the throttle and brakes. A driver coming through a turn low can move wide by increasing his speed via the throttle. Or he can do the reverse by using his brakes. Too much of either will result in a spin. Proper technique involves sliding through the turns, balancing wheel turn, throttle, and brakes.

"The best drivers here back off the throttle a little sooner and get back on it quicker," explains Rick Muther. "Fast times depend on your exit speed, not your entrance speed. Anybody can get through the turn by slamming on his brakes. But they lose speed if they don't know how to get back on the throttle."

Coming out of Turn One, the drivers move within a few feet of the wall each time, then duck low, cutting Turn Two as tightly as possible. Then they slide into the back straightaway, moving up near the wall again. Turns Three and Four are repeats of One and Two.

But not quite. Though identical in their dimensions, each turn requires different handling. Drivers may take one turn tighter, sometimes even below the line, and move higher through others. Nor is one turn the same each day. The wind blowing across the track affects the cars. In Indianapolis in May, the wind usually blows from the west. Turns One and Four are protected from westerly winds by grandstands. The wind can sweep across a half mile of open infield to the other two turns, pushing cars too wide out of Turn Two and too wide into Turn Three. The drivers must adjust their braking points depending on the direction and speed of the wind.

Another car moved from the pits and started building speed, moving low through Turn One. It was blue with a yellow lightning streak and the number 15 on its side. "Fifteen," said one of the fans in Grandstand E.

"Joe Leonard," his friend identified the car correctly. But the helmet barely visible in the cockpit was not the black one of Joe Leonard, but the red one of his teammate, Al Unser. Joe Leonard was in Dallas on business. Al's car number 2 hadn't arrived in town yet, so Al borrowed Joe's for some practice laps.

Soon Al moved up into the groove, and the car wound round and round the dark layer of rubber again and again and again, just like the Johnny Lightning slot cars built by the toy company sponsoring the Unser/Leonard team. Al ran a half dozen laps, each one of them almost identical in speed to the one before. The fastest was 165.1 mph, which tied him with Lloyd Ruby (in car number 12) for fastest lap of the day.

The Unser brothers—Jerry, Louis, Bobby, and Al

If a driver deserved to be named the greatest of all time (GOAT) at the Indianapolis Speedway in 1969, it was not Jigger Sirois but Al Unser. Sirois appeared to be the GOAT because, had he accepted his fourth qualifying lap, he would have sat on the pole. But any other driver or crew chief, given the same set of circumstances, would have acted the same.

Al Unser, on the other hand, had been running fast practice laps all month. Then one evening before qualifications he fell off his motorcycle and broke his leg. Unser reacted calmly: "I guess the accident was meant to happen."

Al Unser came from a racing family. At an age when most kids still rode bicycles, the Unser brothers raced Model A Fords around a dirt track their father built in the back yard. He gave them a gallon of gas each day for practice.

In 1948, the three older Unser brothers began racing. Jerry Unser Jr. drove modified stockcars at age sixteen. The father, meanwhile, began working on a car for Louie. One day, another driver failed to appear for a race, and fourteen-year-old Bobby was offered his car. "When I was sixteen, I won the championships in Albuquerque," recalls Bobby, "and that was the greatest drawing card they had—because I was so young."

Al Unser waited impatiently while his older brothers went racing. One afternoon his parents walked into their backyard garage in time to hear him brag to his brothers: "You guys got nothing on me. I just crashed one!" Ten-year-old Al had rolled the Model A on the family dirt track. When he looked around and saw his parents, his face turned bright red.

"I was too tickled to get really upset," said his mother when she told the story afterward.

Louie, Jerry, and Bobby traveled to Colorado Springs in 1955 to attempt the Pikes Peak Hill Climb. They finished third, fourth, and fifth. They also served as drivers of the tour buses and limousines that took people up and down the mountain. "We used to scare the pants off the tourists," remembers Bobby.

In 1956, Bobby Unser won at Pikes Peak. But Jerry Unser Jr. became the first member of the family to race at the Indianapolis Speedway. He qualified for the 500 in 1958, his first year at the track, and soared over the outside wall in the multicar first lap accident that killed driver Pat O'Connor. Jerry Unser was lucky: he suffered only a dislocated shoulder. At the Speedway the next year he was unlucky: he collided with the wall in practice and died when his car caught fire. Louie Unser retired from racing after being stricken with muscular dystrophy. He now runs an engine shop on the West Coast.

After Bobby Unser's Pikes Peak victory in 1956, he finished fifth the following year. Then he won the race six years in a row. He also set the record for the fastest time up the mountain. In 1964, another driver broke Bobby's record as well as his victory string. It was little brother Al.

Parnelli Jones raced at Pikes Peak in 1962, finished behind Bobby, but talked him into racing the next May in Indianapolis. Parnelli arranged for Bobby to get a ride at the Speedway and helped him through the rookie test. Bobby's car wouldn't go fast enough to qualify, however, so Parnelli walked over to Andy Granatelli's garage and said: "I want you to give Bobby Unser a ride in your car."

"Who's Bobby Unser?" replied Granatelli.

Jim Hurtubise already had qualified one of Andy's Novi racers with a time over 150 miles per hour. Although several drivers had tried, nobody could get one of the other two Novis over 146 mph. On Bobby's fourth lap around the track, he hit 149 mph. Andy hired him, and Bobby easily qualified for the race. In the third lap, however, he spun, placing thirty-third. Bobby drove three years for Andy Granatelli. "I had a lot of fun with the Novis, but my luck was very bad," Bobby recalls. In 1964, he got caught in the fiery second lap accident that killed Eddie Sachs and Dave MacDonald, but he suffered only minor face burns. A broken oil fitting caused him to drop out of the race in 1965.

That year, little brother Al arrived at the Speedway. He felt a pressure beyond that of most rookie drivers. Both Jerry and Bobby had qualified for the race in their first years. Al, however, couldn't get his car rolling fast enough, and late on the last day of qualifications the engine blew. "I was really shook up," Al remembers. "I rushed back to my garage and sat in the corner. I was ready to go home. Everything seemed lost. I had blown my big chance to make my first 500."

At that moment, A. J. Foyt walked in the door and offered Al a ride in one of his backup cars. Unser qualified thirty-second, then finished ninth in the race. Foyt's mechanic at the time was George Bignotti.

Al Unser and Gordon Johncock staged a hot fight for third place in the late stages of the 1966 race. On the 161st lap, Al spun into the inside wall. Graham Hill, the eventual winner, was behind him at the time. Bobby placed eighth, despite a twenty-eight-minute pit stop.

Foyt and Bignotti had parted by then. In 1967, Bignotti hired Al Unser to drive for him. Late in the race, Al held second place but had to make an unscheduled pit stop. "Al was pointing at the car, but he didn't know what was wrong," recalls Bignotti. "We ran around feeling all the tires and finally found that the left rear was flat. He had run over a nail. It cost us forty seconds. Foyt never should have won that race." Al Unser finished second; Bobby took ninth.

The year 1968, however, would belong to Bobby Unser. He qualified for the outside of the front row, the fastest piston car next to two Andy Granatelli turbines. Joe Leonard had set a track record in qualifying for the pole, but Bobby rushed past him on the eighth lap. Unser remained in front most of the way, losing the lead only on pit stops. When he made his third pit stop at 166 laps, Lloyd Ruby and then Joe Leonard moved in front. Then Carl Williams crashed. The leaders bunched together under the yellow flag. When the green light flashed again at 192 laps, Leonard's fuel pump failed. Bobby Unser won that race, the Pikes Peak Hill Climb for the ninth time, and the national championship. In 1969, he placed third at Indianapolis despite five pit stops. Brother Al lost a wheel and crashed in 1968; the next year he broke his leg.

"I really feel that Al is going to be the number one driver in the country," Bobby told Ray Brock, a reporter for *Hot Rod* magazine, after his Indianapolis win. "He will have some bad days, but I think he has natural talent. . . . Al doesn't have the amount of desire he needs, but once he finds out how to win races and has a little luck, he'll get the desire—and then he's going to be untouchable."

Later in the 1969 season, after his leg healed, Al Unser found out how to win. He won five straight championship races in a Lola that George Bignotti had purchased the year before. "I changed all the suspension points and components as we progressed through the season," Bignotti explains. "One of the reasons we started winning was that with the changes we kept sneaking up on the car. We made it a bit better every race we went to."

In November 1969, Al Unser appeared at Indianapolis with several other drivers, including Lloyd Ruby and Art Pollard, to test tires for Firestone. He ran 172.8 mph, faster than the track record. By then he and Bignotti had the backing of Parnelli Jones and Vel Miletich, partners in a West Coast auto agency. For the 1970 season, Parnelli Jones talked Topper Toy Company, makers of the Johnny Lightning racing sets, into sponsoring a two-driver Indianapolis race team.

Lola couldn't supply a new racer, so Bignotti had two cars built in California using the Lola design. The first was completed in March, but snow canceled tire tests scheduled for Indianapolis that month.

On Tuesday, Al Unser stood in the pits watching his teammate test that first car. His own racer was en route from California. Leonard reached 165.6 mph, but Lloyd Ruby had the day's fastest time of 166.9 mph. Mark Donohue appeared and did 165.4 mph. Donnie Allison spun in the first turn but didn't hit the wall. Bentley Warren lost control in the same turn when his radiator cap came off, spraying him with water. Jim Hurtubise also drove his car on the track, the front-engine roadster. Hurtubise was a driver with a past; Al Unser was a driver with a future.

Two rookies: Sam Posey and Bill Simpson

At nine o'clock Wednesday morning, rookies Bill Simpson and Sam Posey, both already dressed in their cream-colored driver's uniforms, stood talking in Gasoline Alley. A small man passed. He wore a yellow Speedway cap and a USAC official's armband.

Simpson recognized the man and called him over. "Have you met Mauri Rose, Sam?"

Posey's face brightened at the mention of the three-time Indianapolis winner's name. "I've certainly heard of you, Mr. Rose," he said. They shook hands.

Posey would begin the first stage of his rookie test that morning: ten laps at 140 miles per hour under the eyes of the track observers. Simpson had driven ten laps each at 140 and 145 mph the two previous days. He was ready for the third stage: ten laps at 150 mph. Finally, he would have to drive ten laps at any faster, "comfortable" speed. For this last stage, several veteran drivers would pass on him. Only then would he receive his Indianapolis license.

"Listen Bill," Rose advised, "take it easy. We'd rather have you do one hundred fifty-one than one hundred sixty." Simpson nodded.

Mauri Rose continued on his way. Sam Posey watched him for a few seconds, then turned back to Simpson: "Gosh, that was Mauri Rose."

Simpson and Posey were but two of twenty-one rookies entered at Indianapolis. Simpson owned a safety equipment business; several of the race cars at Indianapolis used Simpson safety belts. Posey's background was in road racing.

Regardless of a driver's record elsewhere, he wears the label "rookie" at Indianapolis if he has never started a 500 race. Thus, another rookie was Chris Amon, of New Zealand, who had won at Le Mans with Bruce McLaren in 1966.

When the rookies first appear at the Speedway, the other drivers help teach them the track. The veterans do this partly for self-protection: they don't want the rookies wandering and spinning all over the track in front of them.

Later the advice ceases. The rookies must feel their way on a strange track. They must now compete against canny veterans who know every crack in the pavement. The previous year only five rookies qualified in the top thirty-three. In fifty-four Indianapolis races, only four first-year men ever won. One was Ray Harroun in 1911, when the entire field consisted of rookies.

Shortly after the track opened at nine, Kevin Bartlett began the third stage of his rookie test in car number 76, a shiny silver, black, and red model. In Gasoline Alley, a crowd formed around the garages of A. J. Foyt as Foyt waxed his orange Coyote. A station wagon arrived dragging a trailer with the yellow racer of Johnny Rutherford. Denis Hulme consulted with owner Bruce McLaren after several practice laps in car 79, then stepped out and into 75. Dan Gurney sat nearby waiting for a mechanic to return from his garage with a part.

Parked nearby was a yellow car—28. Bill Simpson stood beside it talking with his chief mechanic, Jim Ward, and another crewman. Ward held a squirt can in one hand and wore a red apron with INDIANA OXYGEN COMPANY written across the front. EVERYTHING FOR YOUR NEEDS, it said.

Weld sailed past one more time, his speed now 147.6 mph. The official called to Simpson: "Go run three laps and then come in."

Simpson climbed into his car and headed for the track. Weld rushed past again and was shown he had gone 148.2 mph. Grant King waved at him to slow down. His next lap was 148.7.

Simpson finished the three warm-up laps and returned to the pits, cutting his Chevrolet engine. He sat in the car and waited. Weld finished ten laps at 145 mph and was ready to move to the 150-mph stage. The official on the phone called to Grant King: "They're going to start Simpson's test, so you'll have to pull your man in." King nodded and signaled to wave down Weld.

Simpson had completed seven laps at 150 mph the day before. Then a rocker arm on his engine broke. The officials asked him to do five more laps at that speed. He headed down the runway once more. After two warm-up laps, he came past at 152.3 mph. The crewman marked "52" on a board and held it up the next time he passed. His next two laps were 54 and 55, but as he passed again on a 52 lap a puff of smoke appeared above his engine. Ward threw his arms up in the air: "Looks like he broke another rocker arm."

Simpson coasted back into the pits, removing his helmet as he climbed from the car. "Did we have five?" he asked Ward.

"Four," the mechanic answered.

Simpson took his gloves and slammed them hard into the helmet. He stalked to the pit wall and sat down. "Cool it," Ward told him.

As they began to push the car back toward Gasoline Alley, Donnie Allison moved out into the track driving an orange-colored car from the Foyt stable, number 83. Allison, along with Bartlett and Weld, would complete his rookie test that day. Sam Posey would have to wait until tomorrow.

Simpson, carrying his helmet, began the long walk down the pit wall toward the entrance to Gasoline Alley. The officials later gave him credit for a fifth lap and, after repairs on his car, he would complete his test that day. As Simpson crossed the walkway between the grandstands and Gasoline Alley, a group of boys surrounded him. He signed a number of autographs.

After he had passed, one of the boys glanced at the slip of paper in his hand. "Never heard of him," he said to one of his friends. "Who's Bill Simpson?"

Dan Gurney, Charlie Glotzbach, and some facts about tires

Dan Gurney sat in the cockpit of his Eagle, hands folded before his chin, and regarded calmly the clipboard held by mechanic Wayne Leary. The clipboard showed his speed: 168.5 miles per hour, fastest time of the month. Gurney nodded. His blue eyes, the only part of him visible beneath his mask-like hood and helmet, stared at the numbers. "That's pretty fast," Leary suggested.

"We don't know what fast is yet," said the driver.

Gurney removed the helmet and ran a hand across his straight, blond hair. The thirty-nine-year-old driver had placed second at Indianapolis the two previous years. The last driver to score back-to-back second-place finishes had been Bill Holland in 1947 and 1948. Holland won the next year, a fact that hadn't escaped Gurney's attention. "I'm not interested in setting a record for second-place finishes," he said when he arrived at the track in May.

Dan Gurney grew up in New York (where his father sang with the Metropolitan Opera Company), attended college in California, and volunteered for the Korean War with an antiaircraft gun unit. In 1955, he began racing sports cars and four years later went to Europe to drive for Ferrari. In his first three races he placed second, third, and fourth. Two years later (driving for Porsche) he tied for third in the world championship point standings. In 1967, he and A. J. Foyt became the first American team to win the twenty-four-hour race at Le Mans.

Dan Gurney has had his share of bad luck. His car ran out of fuel only one lap from the finish line while leading the 1964 Belgian Grand Prix. In 1966 at Sebring, his engine failed to start, costing him ninety seconds. In the next nine laps, he passed fifty-four cars but ran out of fuel again, although ahead and 200 yards from the finish. In 1968, *Car & Driver* magazine passed out DAN GURNEY FOR PRESIDENT bumper stickers. He failed to win.

Gurney first came to Indianapolis in 1962, the second driver (after Jack Brabham) to attempt the 500 in a rear-engine car. Gear trouble sidelined him after ninety-three laps. In 1963, Jimmy Clark and Gurney brought the first Ford V-8 engines to the Speedway since 1953. Clark got second, Gurney seventh. Gurney used stock block Ford engines in his 1968 and 1969 second-place finishes, but this May he had arrived in town with a turbo-charged Offy in the back of his newly designed Eagle.

The Eagles, built by Gurney's All American Racers organization in Santa Ana, California, had proved very popular with Indianapolis drivers. In 1968, Eagles driven by Bobby Unser, Gurney, and Denis Hulme placed first, second, and fourth at the 500. More Eagles were entered at Indianapolis in 1970 than any other car.

The new Eagle had a V-bottom like a boat. Generally, air pressure flowing beneath a car causes it to rise, thus slowing it. Gurney hoped the V-shape would push air to the side. He wasn't sure how well the design would work.

The 168.5-mph lap should have encouraged him. But the weather was cool and damp. Dan Gurney realized how much the coolness had helped his speed. He admitted this as he strode back to his garage to escape a light shower: "We're doing it entirely with the engine. I'm not getting around the corners at all."

Mechanic Jim Ward squatted on an oil can before Bill Simpson's garage, smoking a cigar and drinking a soft drink. The engine had been removed from car number 28. Earlier in the morning he had driven Simpson to the airport. "He had to get back home to his shop," Ward explained. "He can't spend all month here. Look at this weather. It's another day wasted."

* * *

Throughout the month several Indianapolis drivers would spend as much time in planes as in their race cars. Denis Hulme, Chris Amon, and Bruce McLaren had left the day before to fly to the Grand Prix in Monaco. Mark Donohue would leave later that day to drive in a Trans-American race in Lime Rock, Connecticut. Gurney and Sam Posey also would race at Lime Rock. Yesterday Charlie Glotzbach had flown to Darlington, South Carolina, where he qualified fastest for Saturday's Rebel 400.

The rain stopped and the sun appeared around one o'clock. Glotzbach, wearing a plum-purple jacket with yellow racing stripes, leaned against his garage door and watched his chief mechanic, Dick Oeffinger, change the sparkplugs of the Weinberger Homes Special, car number 45.

Two racing fans passed the garage. "Hey Charlie," one of them called out, "congratulations on winning the pole [at Darlington]."

Charlie Glotzbach thanked them.

"We'd sure like to see you win the pole *here*," said one of the fans. Charlie smiled.

Oeffinger motioned to one of his crewmen to move the starter into place. The starter whined and the engine caught. Oeffinger massaged the throttle gently: *RUMMM. RUMMMM. RUMMMMM.* Soon a crowd, attracted by the sound, stood watching.

"Attention in the garage area," said the loudspeaker. "The track is now open for practice."

Oeffinger cut the engine and began removing the plugs. (Race mechanics use one type of plug for warming up their engines and another "hotter" set for racing.) Charlie Glotzbach walked over toward him, unzipping his purple jacket.

"About ready, huh?"

Oeffinger nodded. "Better go in there and get your uniform on."

Two crewmen helped Dick Oeffinger push the car toward the track. The Gasoline Alley gate slid open. The gate guards sounded their whistles, warning people out of the way as the car was rolled into the passageway between the grandstands. It stopped near the Goodyear garage. A Goodyear engineer walked around the car with a tire gauge checking pressures.

Front tires on Indianapolis cars are ten inches wide. The rear power wheels have fourteen-inch-wide tires. Drivers in a 500 race make eight hundred turns to the left. ("If you turn right," Bill Vukovich used to say, "you're in trouble.") Since this places more load on the outside wheels, particularly on the right rear wheel, tire pressures vary. The left front tire might contain twenty-four pounds of pressure and the left rear twenty-eight, whereas the right front and rear tires might have thirty-two and thirty-five pounds.

While the Goodyear engineer checked pressures, Dick Oeffinger pounded the three-spoked hub holding the wheel in place with a mallet, a safety precaution. (Earlier that morning Bentley Warren's left front wheel had spun off as he moved down the backstretch. He skidded a hundred yards before stopping unhurt. Had this happened on a turn, the accident might have been serious.)

Out on the track, Donnie Allison and Art Pollard cruised slowly on the inside.

Charlie Glotzbach removed his purple jacket and climbed into his car. Whistles sounded as Sam Posey rumbled past, headed for the track.

The starter whined. Glotzbach's engine sputtered, then died. He sat in the cockpit gripping the wheel with both hands. This time the engine caught. Charlie reached for the gearshift lever with his right hand and the car moved forward. Oeffinger walked with his crew across the runway to stand by the track wall.

"Good afternoon, ladies and gentlemen," rumbled the loudspeaker. "Welcome to the Indianapolis Motor Speedway. We're with you each afternoon at trackside."

Charlie Glotzbach came rolling past on the inside. The second time around one of his crewmen held up a blackboard lettered with CHARLIE across the top. He came by again and by the fourth pass had moved wide and up into the groove. They showed him the blackboard on the next lap: 59. On his sixth pass, Oeffinger stood by the wall rotating his arm—a signal for Charlie to "wind it up" (go to full speed).

"Now on the track in the Weinberger Home Special," announced the loudspeaker, "car number 45, Charlie Glotzbach."

Tony Adamowicz circled the track too. Mark Donohue did a slow warm-up lap. Lloyd Ruby pulled from the pits in his number 25 car. The crowd of several hundred people applauded loudly.

As Ruby went out, Glotzbach came in. Charlie cut the engine and removed his helmet. He signaled with his palm indicating the ride had been smooth. Oeffinger kneeled beside the cockpit and showed the driver a clipboard with his lap times. The fastest one had been 161.8 mph.

Two Goodyear technicians meanwhile moved swiftly around the car, sticking temperature probes into the tire threads. They poked each tire in three places and recorded the temperatures on a small pad. Oeffinger looked at the slip handed him by the technicians, then showed it to his driver. Glotzbach nodded. The right rear tire was running cooler than the other three. Oeffinger signaled his men to remove the rear cowl so they could adjust the spring settings.

* * *

Both Goodyear and Firestone check temperature readings for the drivers using their tires. They learn whether the tires are running hot or cold. As a tire warms, its rubber in effect melts and becomes stickier. This gives it better traction for gripping the track. However, if a tire gets too hot, the rubber will begin to peel. Then the tire may not last the entire race.

Several factors affect tire temperatures. The first, of course, is the heat of the track itself. But that is the same for all drivers. More critical is how each car handles. The chassis must be tuned so that when a car goes around a turn the weight is balanced among all four wheels. For if the chassis is unbalanced, throwing too much weight onto one wheel, that tire will overheat and may need replacing. Changing tires costs time. Victories often are won in the pits.

Temperatures also may vary from one side of the tire tread to the other. If the left side of the tire is hotter than the middle or the right side, that may mean the tire is toeing out or in. Mechanics check tire temperatures while balancing their cars. They can shift the springs, roll bars, or shock absorbers. They can change the angle of the tires. They can make about a half-dozen adjustments on one wheel to change the ride of the car.

But as they adjust one wheel, it affects the other wheels. And all this is complicated even more by the driving habits of the man in the cockpit.

So, the crews at Indianapolis check the tire temperatures, send their driver out onto the track, then bring him back in. They ask him how the car ran, check tire temperatures, and make more adjustments. They test, adjust, test, adjust, all the time searching for the right combination to make their cars move fast through the turns. This is known as "dialing in" the car. Some crews dial their cars in quickly and run fast times in early May with seemingly little effort. Other crews test and tinker all month and never seem to gain speed. Still others find speed only to lose it. It makes for a long, nervous month, since running fast at Indianapolis takes more than a strong engine and a heavy-footed driver.

* * *

Charlie Glotzbach climbed into his car again and ran a half dozen laps at the speed he had been turning earlier. "We don't need to go much faster than one hundred sixty right now," he said. "Next week we may try to slide it up a bit."

When Oeffinger's crew pushed their car back to Gasoline Alley, they passed Al Unser donning his red helmet. His car finally had arrived from California. Al was eager to try it for size. He settled into his seat and waited while mechanic George Bignotti fastened his shoulder harness. Before the track closed that night, Al Unser sped a lap in 168.8 mph. The time ranked only a tenth of a second slower than the 168.9 posted by Mark Donohue just before he left by jet for Lime Rock, Connecticut.

Lloyd Ruby

Lloyd Ruby sat on the pit wall and stroked his cleft chin with one hand. Brightly colored racing cars flashed by on the track, but he seemed not to see them. A straw cowboy hat shaded his face.

At precisely eleven, Lloyd Ruby rose from the pit wall and placed the straw hat in a nearby electric cart. He was ready to go racing.

Ruby, forty-two years old, from Wichita Falls, Texas, began his racing career driving midget autos in 1946 but didn't arrive at Indianapolis until 1960. In ten years of racing, he had covered 4,167.5 miles—more than any other active driver. But he had never finished first. "No matter how much work you do, you've got to have luck," says Ruby. He has never had it.

In Ruby's rookie year, he was running third late in the race when his fuel tanks ran dry. He eventually finished seventh. The following year he sat next to the pole but placed eighth after stalling his engine trying to avoid an accident on the main straightaway. He got eighth again in 1962. A year later he moved from eighteenth to second, only to spin in his own leaking oil. When told that someone had described him as a charger, Ruby smiled. "That's the only way to race, isn't it?"

He achieved a career high third-place finish in 1964, then blew an engine in 1965. Lloyd's luck turned from bad to rotten the next year. He led by nearly an entire lap at 150 laps; then his car began leaking oil. Parnelli Jones had won in 1963 while leaking oil, and car owner Colin Chapman complained that victory should have gone to his driver, Jim Clark. Officials, remembering the Jones–Clark rhubarb, black-flagged Lloyd Ruby.

In 1967 Ruby crashed. In 1968, he had the lead at 175 laps and had turned the ninety-fourth lap in 168.666 mph, the fastest speed ever recorded during a 500 race. Then a coil malfunctioned. Six minutes later Lloyd returned to the track and charged again, finishing fifth. His actual running time was twenty-seven seconds faster than winner Bobby Unser. Later that year while leading a 200-mile race in Phoenix, Ruby pitted because of a flat rear tire. He zoomed back onto the track again, only to realize that his crew had changed the wrong tire.

Lloyd Ruby blew an engine in 1969 just before his qualification attempt. He qualified the next day in the twentieth spot. During the race he moved up steadily, while A. J. Foyt held the lead. Foyt stopped for fuel and Wally Dallenbach led briefly. Then on lap seventy-nine Foyt had turbocharger problems and Ruby roared past him. He held first place for eight laps. Mario Andretti, who earlier had slowed to keep his engine from overheating, passed him. Ruby regained the lead on lap 103, but Andretti passed him again three laps later. On the 108th lap Ruby pitted and waited impatiently as his crewmen fueled the car. Since Andretti also would have to refuel soon, the lead soon would belong to the one able to spend the least time in the pits.

Ruby saw the crewman remove the left front hose and started to move. But the left *rear* hose remained snagged in the fueling spout. When Ruby pulled away, the side of the tank ripped open. Fuel cascaded out, and with it went Lloyd Ruby's chances for victory. He watched from the sidelines as Mario Andretti took the checkered flag. "I think if we'd kept running, Andretti wouldn't have finished," Ruby said afterward.

Two months later at Dover, Delaware, Ruby's car bottomed out while going over some ripples in the track surface, and he slid into the wall. The car burst into flames. He received second- and third-degree burns on his face and neck, sidelining him for two months.

The scars from that accident—pink against suntanned skin—were plainly visible this morning in May 1970 as Lloyd Ruby readied himself for practice by tying a red bandana over his nose and mouth. He reached for his racing helmet. Like his car, the helmet was red, white, and blue and had a white star on each side.

He climbed into the car and mechanic Dave Laycock bent to fasten his shoulder harnesses. Ruby drove onto the track, and four members of his crew (each dressed in red, white, and blue uniforms) walked across the runway to the track wall. After only one warm-up lap, however, Lloyd Ruby returned to the pits because of a yellow light. He climbed out of the car, removed his helmet, and retrieved his straw hat from the electric cart. Then he sat down on the pit wall again and waited for his luck to change.

In Gasoline Alley, the previously locked doors to the STP garages swung open. Three mechanics pushed out a bright red car with number 1 on its side and turned it toward the fuel pumps. Several fans began to follow the car, eager to see Andy Granatelli's new entry. Granatelli had hired Francis McNamara of Lengries, Germany, to design a new car for his driver, Mario Andretti.

But the car was merely the Hawk that Lloyd Ruby had watched Andretti drive to victory last year. The McNamara arrival had been delayed by a truck strike. After the crew fueled the Hawk for technical inspection, they pushed it back to the garage and covered it with a red tarpaulin.

In the late afternoon the sun burned down, and the temperature rose to eighty-five degrees. Art Pollard, pitting after a practice run, halted his car so the shadow of the scoring pylon fell across his cockpit. It was the only shade in the entire pit area. Pollard, being a veteran, knew exactly where to find it.

Rick Muther, wearing a floral-patterned shirt outside his jeans, gazed at a stopwatch as his teammate Jigger Sirois rolled past in the Offy-powered car 72. Muther frowned.

The track guards whistled as the Johnny Lightning Special number 2 roared into the pits and slid to a halt. George Bignotti and his crew wore smiles brighter than the sun. Bignotti's watch indicated that Al Unser had covered his last lap at 169.1 miles per hour.

Unser actually had been clocked by the track's electric eye at a speed of 168.792 mph, but as the crew pushed his lightning-striped blue and yellow racer back to its garage, they didn't seem interested in arguing over a few tenths of a second. The big prize would go to the fastest driver on the *thirtieth* of the month.

At five thirty a half dozen reporters were sitting around the press room, when someone walked in to announce: "A jet plane just buzzed the track, and it had the biggest STP sticker I ever saw on its bottom."

Andy Granatelli had arrived in Indianapolis.

Andy Granatelli, Mr. STP

Those present the previous Memorial Day in Indianapolis remembered the look of joy on car owner Andy Granatelli's face when the checkered flag flashed. He started south down the runway toward victory lane wearing his bright red STP jacket. Despite his size, he ran. Three hundred thousand people cheered. Then in one great moment of truth, Andy Granatelli bent and kissed Mario Andretti on the cheek.

Andy joked about that moment afterward. "You probably wonder how I could kiss Mario in front of the whole world," he told banquet audiences. "If you were born of Italian parents, had spent eight million dollars and twenty-three years trying to win the 500, and an Italian driver wins it for you—what other choice do you have?"

Andy Granatelli's father migrated from northern Italy to the United States at age eighteen seeking his fortune. He succeeded as a grocer in Dallas, then the Depression struck. The Granatellis drifted from Chicago to California and back to Chicago, sometimes existing on chicken feed and dandelions.

Andy's mother died when he was twelve. He and his brothers, Joe and Vince, earned money reselling bottles. They peddled vegetables in back alleys. They sold coal, hauling it up stairs in buckets. The brothers also functioned as part-time mechanics. "My father couldn't change a tire," recalls Andy, "but we had a natural feel for automobiles. If someone wanted a transmission fixed, we'd park in front of the auto repair shop, get under the car and do the job on the street."

After World War II, the Granatelli brothers opened a garage selling speed equipment and building cars for hot rodders. They once built a rocket car, sticking eight JATO rockets in the back of a 1934 Ford. It went 180 miles per hour on a back highway. ANTONIO THE GREAT, proclaimed county fair billboards. WORLD-FAMOUS ITALIAN SPEED ACE.

Andy's racing career was short but spirited. Once, while pushing his motorcycle seventy mph through Chicago city streets, he caught the front wheel on some streetcar tracks, flipped over the handlebars, and was run over by his own cycle.

In 1948, after several years driving hot rods, Andy attempted to qualify at Indianapolis, but a tire shredded. His car slammed into the wall, flipped upside down, and skidded along the top of the wall for 300 yards before tumbling back to the track upright. Andy had broken one arm, one hand, two ribs, fractured his skull, lost eleven teeth, and both collarbones had come unhitched near the thyroid gland.

The following September, Andy was sleeping in a car while being driven home from an Indianapolis hot rod show, when a farmer towing a wagon pulled out of a driveway. The car and wagon collided, flipping Andy through the window and seventy-five feet beyond. He landed in a cornfield with another fractured skull, a broken hand, and a broken leg.

Andy Granatelli's back still pains him. He claims that injuries from his accidents caused the glandular troubles responsible for his being overweight. He dislikes excessive heat and keeps his office cooled to sixty-five degrees. Cigarette smoke irritates his sinuses, so he designed the interior of the STP corporate jet without ashtrays. "Anybody who smokes," he says, "buys the plane. That's two million dollars, list price."

Andy's frustrations at Indianapolis began in 1946. The Granatelli brothers first appeared at the Speedway with an outmoded two-seat racer. They drove it to the track because they couldn't afford a trailer. "No car in the history of the 500 ever had license plates on it before," claims Andy. The car qualified at 118.890 mph, but its engine died on the backstretch following a pit stop. The driver had forgotten to reset the fuel shutoff valve. Andy restarted the car, but it already had been disqualified. This misfortune seemed to set the tone for Granatelli's Indianapolis efforts.

The Granatellis brought a car to the track each of the next eight years, placing second in 1952 with Jim Rathmann. Their off-track activities prospered because of the publicity earned in racing. By 1956, their speed business (Grancor for Granatelli Corporation) was earning $14 million annually. The Granatellis had skipped the 1955 race, and they soon sold Grancor. Andy moved to Escondido, California, a retired millionaire at age thirty-four.

The retirement lasted only a few months. Soon he was breaking ground for a bowling alley. In 1958, he purchased Paxton Products, a West Coast supercharger plant which merged into the Studebaker Corporation in 1961. Andy and his brothers went to Studebaker along with Paxton Products. That same year Andy returned to the Speedway.

He purchased the famed eight-cylinder Novi racing cars designed by Ed Winfield. Race fans loved the Novis because of the bellowing roar from their supercharged engines. Nobody before had won with the Novis, nor did Andy during several years' attempts. But meanwhile, he became president of Studebaker's chemical compound division, which produced STP. In 1966, STP backed Jimmy Clark in a rear-engine Lotus Ford. Clark seemingly led the race through the 192nd lap, when suddenly the scoreboard showed Graham Hill in front. The officials had overlooked one of Hill's previous laps. Andy remains unconvinced. "I won the race that year," he says.

The following year marked the debut of the turbine car, the so-called Silent Screamer. Turbine engines originally had been designed for airplanes; no passenger cars used them. The Novis had been the loudest cars on the track; now Andy had appeared with the quietest. It also was the fastest. With Parnelli Jones driving, the STP turbine car held the lead until three laps to go when a six-dollar ball bearing failed.

Andy returned in 1968, despite rule restrictions aimed at his turbine, and qualified three cars. One hit the wall midway through the race. Two others fell out in the closing laps with pump shaft failures. Following the 1968 race, the United States Auto Club tightened the rules once more, so Andy abandoned the turbine.

Bad luck continued to dog Andy Granatelli at Indianapolis in 1969. He signed Mario Andretti as a driver, but Mario crashed his racing car in practice. Mario then stepped into his backup car, a Hawk built by chief mechanic Clint Brawner. He qualified it for the front row between A. J. Foyt and Bobby Unser, the previous year's winner. During the race, one by one the thirty-three starters crashed or failed mechanically, including two from the STP team. Mario Andretti, however, persevered. He won the victory that had eluded his owner for so long.

Now, on the ninth day of the following May, Andy Granatelli stood in the pits late in the afternoon and watched Mario Andretti circle the track in the Hawk at speeds under 160 mph. The Hawk had been completely rebuilt, but the STP team planned to use it only as a backup machine. Their number one car would be the new McNamara.

Earlier in the morning rookie Donnie Allison slammed into the outside wall when a heavy gust of wind pushed him too high coming through the Turn Three. The crash severely damaged the front of the Foyt-sponsored car number 83. Foyt, who had burned two pistons on his own car on Thursday, didn't look very happy. Al Unser and Lloyd Ruby decided against practicing because of the high winds. Roger McCluskey had the day's fastest time with 166.1 mph.

* * *

While Indy was preparing for the 500, the participating drivers were also racing in other events all around the country. For example, on May 9 in Darlington, South Carolina, Charlie Glotzbach led the Charlotte 400 for four laps but failed to finish, as did Lee Roy Yarbrough. At Lime Rock, Connecticut, Sam Posey, who had won that Trans-Am race the year before, placed third. Parnelli Jones, owner of the Johnny Lightning cars, took first. Mark Donohue, Peter Revson, and Dan Gurney failed to finish.

* * *

Back at Indianapolis, Andy Granatelli moved from the track to his garage and finally to the parking lot, where he climbed into a black limousine bearing Illinois license plates AG 500. Several months earlier a radio interviewer had asked him when he planned to quit. "Quit?" responded the man from STP. "I spent twenty-three years at the Speedway and only won one race. Until I get twenty-two more wins, I won't even be even."

Rolla Vollstedt, the high cost of racing, and some prizes

Rolla Vollstedt glanced up while working in his garage in Gasoline Alley. David Blackmer, an Indianapolis public relations man, had shouted hello from outside the fence. Vollstedt walked over to chat.

"I come here five or six weeks a year," explained Vollstedt. "If I put that much extra time into my lumber business, I could afford what it costs me to race here."

Consider the costs of going first class at Indianapolis.

A good race car chassis costs $25,000. A secondhand chassis can be purchased for around $10,000, but nobody wins at Indianapolis (and few even qualify) in a secondhand chassis. The costs of designing a new chassis (such as Andretti's new McNamara or Gurney's latest Eagle) may run to $100,000.

The cost of a turbocharged Ford engine is $28,875. An Offenhauser costs slightly less. You can save roughly $10,000 by purchasing an unblown engine, but you will lose horsepower, about eight miles per hour, and any chance of qualifying.

A first-class racing team will buy two, possibly three, engines per car. They will use one engine for practice, one for qualifying, and one for race day. If an engine blows, because of poor timing or maybe only because of a change in humidity, the repair bill may run as high as $10,000. It will cost $3,000 to $5,000 to overhaul the engine after a race.

That doesn't include tires, which come free if you're Mario Andretti but cost $100 each if you happen to be an unknown.

Many teams have at least one backup car. More often there will be two cars plus a backup model. The cost of three cars and a half dozen engines comes to $200,000.

But nobody yet has designed an Indy car capable of driving itself. The dozen or so top drivers usually sign with a racing team for the entire year and receive a $25,000 salary just for sitting in the cockpit. In addition, they collect 40 percent of any prizes they win. Mario Andretti supposedly receives a basic $100,000 salary, plus 50 percent of what he wins, plus a share of the sponsor fees. In 1967, when Parnelli Jones drove the Granatelli turbine car at Indianapolis, Andy reportedly paid him $75,000 for that single race. An Indianapolis driver also may get a bonus as high as $5,000 if he qualifies. The winner of the 1970 race would receive a $30,000 bonus at the finish line from his sponsoring company.

A second-car driver gets less than his teammate. A big-name driver such as Joe Leonard or Donnie Allison might receive $5,000 to $10,000 for the month in addition to 40 percent of the winnings. A lesser driver would be handed $1,000 plus the percentage.

Some drivers spend the entire month at the Speedway without pay, hoping for a share of any prize money they win. Thirty-third place in the 500 earns more than $12,000; the driver's share would be $4,800. In 1969, Rick Muther received the $500 Dale Mueller consolation award for being the thirty-fourth fastest driver. That money was the difference between his flying and hitchhiking home.

The crew also must be paid. Most first-class teams will employ a dozen men. Some will work only the month of May. Full-time team members earn up to $10,000 a year. A chief mechanic earns at least that much plus 10 percent of all prizes. The best ones earn $25,000 plus 25 percent. The rest of the crew may divide another 10 percent of anything won. In 1968, Andy Granatelli admitted that winning would have cost him more money than losing. He had promised away more than 100 percent of the prize money.

It costs $7,500 to house a crew and feed them. A half dozen passenger cars ($90 a week rental) will be needed to move crew, drivers, and owner around town. A public relations man will easily spend $1,000, not including his salary. The entry fee at Indianapolis is $1,000 per car, multiplied by two or three cars.

With the cost of racing so high, why go racing at all? But while money goes out, it also comes in. Most of the $250,000 McLaren bill was being picked up by three sponsors: Goodyear, Gulf Oil, and Reynolds Aluminum. The better drivers have sponsorships from one of the tire companies. Most important, these companies hire them at other times of the year to test tires at the Speedway. This gives drivers such as Andretti, Foyt, Donohue, Ruby, and the Unsers a large edge over others who only see the track in May.

Business firms pay to have their names displayed on the side of racers. Equipment companies provide free shock absorbers, batteries, tractors, driving uniforms, and helmets. Drivers can get their wheels balanced at the Bear garage for nothing. Magnaflux will examine any parts to detect flaws. Gasoline companies such as Gulf and Ashland provide free fuel, even though they sometimes must buy the methanol from other suppliers.

Many companies also post contingency money for drivers who place high using their products. A Champion sparkplug user, for example, will receive $7,000 for winning. Other front finishers win lesser prizes, sliding down to $100 for twelfth. Indianapolis racers have ten or twenty stickers pasted on their sides naming various sponsors.

It would be difficult to judge the value of such advertising, but a full-page ad in *Sports Illustrated* costs $22,570. The sponsor of the winning 1970 car would see his product name photographed on the cover of that magazine. The previous year, when Mario Andretti pulled into victory circle, an announcer stuck a microphone in his face and asked him why he had won. Mario answered: "I guess we used more STP in our Ford engine than the other drivers." More STP cans were sold the following month than during the entire year of 1962, Andy Granatelli's first year as president of the company.

On the tenth day of May, the price of racing suddenly increased for Rolla Vollstedt. The time was 5:17 p.m. Al Unser had gone 170.9 mph only a few minutes before, and later Art Pollard would post a 169.1 speed. Bruce Walkup passed Vollstedt's driver John Cannon on the main straightaway. Cannon moved into Walkup's slipstream, hoping to improve his speed.

But as the two cars reached the turn, Walkup slowed, and Cannon found himself closing too fast. Cannon moved wide, braked, and began a slow spin. Cannon said later: "I was on the brakes during the spin when I remembered everybody saying, don't do that. So, I got off the brakes, and that's when I went right into the wall."

Gary Bettenhausen and Billy Vukovich

A blue wedge-shaped car coasted into the pits. The driver lifted himself out of the cockpit and removed his helmet with the name GARY lettered on the side. Gary Bettenhausen was at the Speedway for his third year.

He had a reputation as a charger. As a rookie Gary Bettenhausen had moved from twenty-second to ninth in forty-three laps. Then a bouncing part from Al Unser's accident damaged his oil cooler. In 1969 he started ninth. By lap thirty-six he had reached fourth place, when a burned piston halted him.

"If I had known the piston was going to burn," he grumbled afterward, "I would have charged and tried to lead."

Gary Bettenhausen removed his helmet and gloves, setting them in the cockpit. He untied the red bandana from over his mouth and used it to wipe his forehead. It was hot. His car had arrived on Saturday, and he had it up to only 162 miles per hour, too slow for a charger.

Gary's father, Tony Bettenhausen, had raced at Indianapolis fifteen times, taking second in 1955.

Then came 1961. When Tony Bettenhausen left for the Speedway that year his wife, Valerie, made him promise not to drive any car but his own. But the day before qualifications began, Paul Russo asked Tony to check his roadster. As Bettenhausen raced down the main straightaway, a steering cotter pin worked loose. The car veered toward the outside wall, hit it, flew 150 yards, and landed upside down. Before this, Tony Bettenhausen claimed to have been upside down twenty-eight times. But he failed to survive the twenty-ninth time.

Gary was only nineteen when his father was killed. He began racing that same year. When he arrived at the Speedway in 1968, it was to fulfill the desire of his father: that some day the name Bettenhausen would be listed among the winners of the Indianapolis 500.

"I think I can win it," he said now, in 1970. "Maybe eighty percent of the guys in the race will be stroking, trying to finish. Only a handful of the drivers charge, and among them the one who lasts is the one who wins." (In 1969, Gary had won the USAC sprint car championships.)

Gary turned from his car and watched Charlie Glotzbach drive past toward the track. Bentley Warren, another rookie, followed. Gary waited until the two cars passed, then crossed the runway to the strip of grass next to the track. Billy Vukovich, wearing sunglasses and a wide-brimmed yellow Wynn's hat, sat in the grass with his back against the track wall smoking nervously. Gary sat down and borrowed a cigarette.

Like Gary Bettenhausen, Billy Vukovich was the son of a famous race driver. A broken steering pin had caused the crash that ended his father, Bill Vukovich's, life. It happened in 1955, as he tried for his third straight victory.

* * *

Billy first met Gary while both were young kids following their fathers from track to track. Gary's first year at the Speedway was also Billy's, but whereas Gary failed to finish, Billy placed seventh (despite spinning once) and earned Rookie of the Year honors. In 1969, he completed only one lap.

Even more than Gary, Billy felt the pressure of his father's racing success. Perhaps it was because Vukovich's fame exceeded that of Bettenhausen's. "He was a great driver," says Billy, "and I'm proud of my father's achievements. But when people again and again ask questions about him, I sometimes want to scream."

Billy Vukovich has a reputation for a fiery temper. In March at the Houston Astrodome, he held the lead in a midget auto race over A. J. Foyt in the Astro Grand Prix. Ruts soon developed on the turns and Billy, with other drivers, began to cut the turns. As the race progressed, they cut deeper and deeper into the infield. Finally, USAC officials stopped the race.

Vukovich and Foyt started an angry shouting match. When a USAC official tried to interrupt, Vuky told him off. As a result, Billy Vukovich was placed on probation for a year.

As he sat on the grass at Indianapolis, Gary Bettenhausen looked unhappy because of his car's slowness. Billy Vukovich had more reason for anger. He had arrived at Indianapolis ready to run on the first day of May with a car specially built for him. He had not yet broken 160 mph with it. The two sons of famous men sat and smoked and talked.

One of Gary's crew members shouted that his car was ready to go. He crossed the runway. As he picked up his helmet, the loudspeaker crackled: "The yellow light is on."

Bettenhausen threw the helmet back into the cockpit. He sat down on the pit wall with a wry grimace. Vukovich, still watching from the grass, laughed.

The yellow light had come on at 11:21 a.m. because Charlie Glotzbach had spun. He slid 400 feet between Turns Three and Four, but he struck nothing and continued into the pits.

Three hours later almost to the minute, Glotzbach spun again, this time sliding 200 feet between Turns One and Two. The notice on the pressroom blackboard noted wryly that Glotzbach's total footage for the day had been 600 feet.

Two more drivers would earn notices on that blackboard before the day ended. A half hour after Glotzbach's second accident, Kevin Bartlett looped once coming through Turn Two but made no contact. Then at four o'clock a bearing froze in the right rear hubcap of Mario Andretti's new McNamara. He had gotten it onto the track only the day before. The frozen bearing caused a shaft to snap as Mario came out of Turn Four.

He slid toward the inside wall and struck it once, then twice. The impact severely damaged the car; Mario was unhurt. Only a year before, Mario Andretti had crashed while practicing in a new Lola. "I didn't believe it when it happened," the driver remarked afterward. "Same place, practically the same part, same circumstances. Something like that shatters you in every direction."

"Part of the magic of Indianapolis is the fear," Billy Vukovich had told reporter Joe Hamelin of the Indianapolis *Star* a week earlier. "Fear has intimidated and ultimately ruined drivers who excel elsewhere in racing. I think some people are simply afraid of this place, of the speed, of what it can do to you."

Fear later would become a major factor in preventing at least one of the drivers who spun on Monday from succeeding at Indianapolis this year.

Denis Hulme of the McLaren team

The track, still damp from rain, didn't open until midmorning. In the Granatelli garage, five men in freshly laundered STP uniforms hovered around the shell of a racing machine like surgeons around an operating table.

The basic chassis of Mario Andretti's McNamara car was an aluminum monocoque, or "tub." The driver sits—or rather half lies—in the middle of the tub. The engine is bolted to the rear wall behind him. Ahead and behind are attached wheels, springs, gears, instruments: all the hundreds of little parts that make a tub into an automobile.

The impact of Andretti's crash bent the monocoque so it couldn't be repaired. Andy Granatelli, meanwhile, had a second tub (plus enough parts to construct another racer) parked in a rental truck at the Speedway. He and Mario had two options: go with the Hawk, a proven winner, or attempt to ready a second McNamara before qualifications on Saturday.

They chose the second option. The Hawk was outdated. Next to winning, Andy Granatelli likes innovating the most. So, the STP crew accepted the task of building a car from a trailer full of parts. "We have to do in four days," said Andy, with his usual flair for drama, "what originally took us four months."

Mario Andretti hung around the garage, sipped a soft drink, and paced. Vince Granatelli, one of Andy's brothers, asked him to step into the car. Mario removed his shoes and did so. Being fitted to a race car is somewhat like being fitted for a custom suit. One of the mechanics made some measurements and Mario climbed out.

"Hey, Mario," a race fan called from outside the garage. Mario came out and signed several autographs. He posed for a picture. Then he went back inside the garage and paced.

Team McLaren, meanwhile, was out on the track turning lap after lap. Following the Monaco race, Bruce McLaren remained in Europe for several days. Denis Hulme and Chris Amon returned to Indianapolis.

Amon was having trouble learning the track. One day, after being passed by Dan Gurney, Amon slipped in behind him. By drafting Gurney, Amon could move through the turns faster, but as soon as Gurney left the track Amon's speed dropped again.

Hulme had no such troubles. The balding New Zealander had placed fourth twice in three years at Indianapolis. He tried all three McLaren cars, hitting 167.9 in car 75 and 166.9 in 79.

Shortly before three o'clock, the McLaren crew refueled 79. The car had just had an additional safety retaining spring installed on the fuel breather caps. Hulme readied himself to go racing. He wore leather shoes and the standard fireproof Nomex racing uniform used by all the drivers.

He pulled a Nomex hood over his head. Only his nose and eyes peeked through. He donned a crash helmet that completely covered his head. Its plastic visor was tinted a dark green. He pulled on a pair of leather, Nomex-lined racing gloves. Hulme settled into the cockpit of his car. Crew chief Tyler Alexander bent to help fasten his shoulder harness.

Denis Hulme moved onto the track. By the backstretch of his second lap, he was moving full speed. Just before he reached Turn Three, Hulme saw liquid rushing past the left side of the cockpit. Vibration from the new retaining spring had loosened the fuel breather cap.

Hulme immediately recognized the danger. He hit the brakes. He figured the fuel would flow onto the left rear wheel and cause a skid. Instead, the fuel sprayed across the hot turbocharger engine behind him.

On Turn Three, a track observer saw the fuel leak. He instantly pushed the yellow light button. At the same moment he shouted "Fire!"

into his telephone. Around the track, firemen and ambulance attendants jumped into their machines, even while car 79 skidded into the turn.

The instant the fuel sprayed across the turbocharger it ignited. Flames rushed forward and engulfed the cockpit. For an instant, Hulme thought about continuing around the track to the fire engine parked on Turn Four. But the flames might kill him before he rolled that far.

The plexiglass windshield began to melt from the heat, its droppings falling inside the car. The heat also fused the plastic visor to Hulme's helmet. But he still could see, and his helmet permitted him to breathe.

The car contained a fire extinguisher, but Hulme couldn't find the switch. He turned the car left, hoping it was going around the corner, and continued braking. He knocked the car out of gear and hit the ignition switch, killing the engine. All this happened within seconds, and meanwhile the car continued to slide through the Turn Three.

Hulme got ready to abandon the car. He fumbled with his seat belt release. His hands hurt. The belts finally came loose. Because he knew the left side of the car was on fire, Hulme jumped from the right side. He had no idea how fast the car was going.

He landed on his left side and rolled. Luckily his car had almost come to a stop. It continued toward the infield and bounced against a concrete wall.

The fall hadn't injured Hulme, and he climbed to his feet in time to see Ronnie Bucknum zoom past him on the outside. He began to run toward his car, hoping to help put out the fire, but firemen already were spraying it with chemicals.

The ambulance arrived and Denis Hulme climbed into the back. At the field hospital, the doctors cut the gloves off his hands. The intense heat had shrunk the leather, causing second- and third-degree burns. The same happened with his leather shoes.

The safety equipment worn by Denis Hulme probably saved his life, but he spent the next two weeks in the hospital. Another month would pass before he raced again. Ironically, the accident had occurred because of the addition of a device (the retaining spring) designed to make the car safe.

May 13, Wednesday

A driver without a car, a racing film, and Johnny Rutherford

The rains fell again Wednesday morning. Inside a trailer belonging to Art Pollard, a group of men sat and talked about a film for STP.

The door opened and a man in a tan raincoat walked in. His hair lay wet across his forehead. It was driver George Follmer. "Anyone seen Art?" he asked.

No one had. Follmer left and returned ten minutes later. He accepted an offer to sit down.

Film producer Al Blanchard was describing how his crew photographed the Indianapolis 500. Blanchard used eight cameramen for qualifications and a dozen men on race day. Three worked in the pits. The rest stationed themselves around the track, both on the outside and inside. Blanchard would shoot 20,000 feet of film but could use only 800 feet in the half-hour movie he was producing for STP.

"We'll get as much film as possible on our cars," explained Blanchard. "But we film the entire race as well. You can't shoot all the time, but we're alert for any car that gets out of shape and looks as though it might crash."

George Follmer sat on a sofa, nervously drumming his fingers on his knees. He still wore his raincoat.

An STP vice president discussed Mario Andretti's accident two days before: "The clouds were getting dark when they rolled the car out. Mario took one warm-up lap and on the second lap he hit the wall. Suddenly there was a big flash of lightning, followed by a crash of thunder. It was quite dramatic, almost as though he had been struck by fate."

Follmer sat and drummed. He had started the 500 in 1969, but this year he did not yet have a ride. It is embarrassing for a race driver to sit idle during the month of May. So Follmer hung around Art Pollard, who had an extra backup car. Pollard was noncommittal. Follmer also talked with Andy Granatelli about Andretti's old Hawk. Andy told George maybe. That was before Mario crashed the new McNamara.

"We're working steadily around the clock on Mario's car," the STP vice president explained to TV announcer Jim Wilson. "We hope to have it ready by late afternoon or tonight. That gives us Thursday and Friday to set it up for the track. If we can even attempt to qualify, it's a miracle. We'll take the best time we can get, then try to build up speed the next week."

"What speed will you accept?" asked Wilson.

"I think it will take one hundred sixty-five to make the race."

George Follmer rose from the sofa and said he thought he'd look around for Pollard. After he left, Wilson asked about Follmer's chances of getting the Hawk.

The STP vice president explained that Andy had made no promises. "We've hardly touched the car since Mario ran it last month in Trenton."

When the rain stopped after noon, the drivers rushed to the track to recapture lost practice time. Kevin Bartlett roared loudly down the straightaway. A. J. Foyt stood by the pit watching George Snider pass in one of Foyt's racers. Jim Malloy waited while mechanics adjusted the blower pressure on his turbocharged Offenhauser engine. The yellow light flashed: Johnny Rutherford's nose cone had come off on the back straightaway. Rutherford pulled into the pits and walked to his garage in disgust.

On January 20, Johnny Rutherford (along with Lee Roy Yarbrough) had been the first driver to officially enter the Indianapolis 500. His luck at the Speedway had been poor: in six starts he never had finished.

The thirty-two-year-old driver from Fort Worth, Texas, had lasted only forty-three laps in 1963, his first year. The following May, with less than two laps completed, he got caught in the fiery crash that killed

Dave MacDonald and Eddie Sachs. Driving through the flames, Rutherford was hit broadside by Bobby Unser's Novi. He suffered only minor burns, but his car was too badly damaged to continue. In 1965, a year in which he won the USAC sprint car championships, Rutherford's rear-end gear failed at fifteen laps.

One month before the Speedway opened in 1966, Rutherford flipped over the outside guard rail in a sprint car race in Rossburg, Ohio. He broke both arms and didn't race again until the next 500 race. He hit the inside rail on the 104th lap.

Rutherford burned one hand severely in a crash at Phoenix in April 1968. At the Speedway he was hit from behind by Jimmy McElreath while trying to avoid Billy Vukovich's spinning car. A split oil tank forced him from the 1969 race after twenty-four laps.

Now it looked like another bad month for Johnny Rutherford. When he first arrived at the Speedway, Rutherford had hit 163 miles per hour. His car handled smoothly. Then Rutherford and mechanic Mike Devin began adjusting the chassis. The more they tinkered, the slower the car got. On Wednesday they found themselves still unable to find the right settings. After his crew replaced the nose cone, Rutherford returned to the track for more practice laps. He couldn't force the car any faster than 161 mph.

Rutherford stood beside his car glumly staring at it. "I guess we'd better set everything back to zero," said Devin, "and start all over again."

Chris Amon of the McLaren team also was wondering why he had agreed to come to Indianapolis. His best speed that day was 162.1 mph. With Denis Hulme hospitalized, he now had a new partner: Peter Revson, a thirty-one-year-old bachelor. Revson's family controlled Revlon, Inc., the beauty products firm.

Last year Revson had qualified thirty-third and finished fifth as a rookie. He had come to Indianapolis this year with another car. When Bruce McLaren asked him to replace Hulme, he quickly said yes. In his first day in Hulme's car, Revson clocked 166.4 mph. This did little to boost Chris Amon's ego.

Sam Posey, however, was bubbling. He drove into the pits with a broad grin on his face. He had just gone 166.0 mph. Posey seemed certain to qualify on Saturday.

Mario Andretti and the new McNamara

Long before the first fan arrived on Thursday, the doors of the STP garage stood open. They had closed rarely during the last three days, as the Granatelli crew worked to ready Mario Andretti's McNamara. Mario's old Hawk stood neglected nearby, covered by a red tarpaulin.

By the time Andy Granatelli arrived shortly after nine, the McNamara car had begun to take shape. Andy carried his gray suit coat slung over one shoulder.

He paused beside the Hawk. One of his mechanics was removing the tarpaulin. The Hawk lay bare, its engine missing. "We're going to shove the engine in now, right?" said Andy.

The mechanic said yes. Vince Granatelli had been supervising work on the McNamara. Andy's other brother, Joe, would arrive in town today to work on the Hawk. George Follmer still might get his chance.

Ten minutes later Mario Andretti arrived dressed in bell-bottomed trousers and a tan coat with ringed zippers. He glanced under the car to check the progress of the work. The previous year he had won more than $350,000 in prize money and probably earned at least that much more through endorsements and public appearances.

In contrast to the rich STP operation, Jerry Karl worked next door with one other crewman adjusting his engine. The nose of his racer was dented, its paint job faded. While trying to pass his rookie test, Karl had blown two engines. If it happened one more time, he could go home for the month.

It had been that way once for Mario Andretti.

He was born in 1940 near Trieste. After World War II the Andrettis left their home and spent seven years living in Italian displaced persons camps. At age thirteen Mario and his twin brother Aldo talked a garage owner in the town of Lucca into letting them park cars—even before they had learned to drive. "The first time I fired up an engine I was hooked," recalls Mario today. "I still get that feeling every time I get into a race car."

He and Aldo bought a motorcycle, then began driving 85-horse-power cars—without telling their father. Mario idolized the Italian driving champion Alberto Ascari and first heard of the Indianapolis 500 because Ascari raced there in 1952.

In 1955, the Andretti family moved to Nazareth, Pennsylvania. Mario and Aldo still wanted to become race drivers. In 1959, they rebuilt a 1948 Hudson Hornet and flipped a coin to see who would race first. Aldo won the coin flip and the race. The next weekend Mario drove the car, winning his first race—and ninety dollars in prize money.

The twin brothers still hadn't informed Papa Andretti. Late that year at Hatfield, Pennsylvania, Aldo hooked the guard rail and demolished the Hornet, and almost himself. He fractured his skull and remained in a coma for two weeks. When he began talking, Aldo's first words were: "I'm glad you were the one who had to go home and face the old man."

Aldo recovered slowly but raced again. In 1969, he flipped in a sprint car and shattered his face against a steel mesh fence. After that, he decided to retire. "Whenever I look at the Unser brothers," says Mario, "I can't help but think that, except for a twist of fate, that could be us."

Mechanic Clint Brawner discovered Mario driving sprint cars in 1964 and brought him to the Speedway the following year. Though he finished third, Mario was hardly content. "Third place is complete defeat," he said. "Second place is complete defeat. First place is all that is worth anything."

Mario won the USAC championship point title that year, becoming at age twenty-five the youngest national champ ever (by six weeks over A. J. Foyt). Shortly afterward he appeared on the Joey Bishop television program. Bishop introduced Andretti as "rookie of the year at Indian-apolis." Mario realized that to be accepted as number one, he would have to win the 500.

The next three years he qualified for the pole twice but completed a total of only eighty-seven laps. In 1969, he signed a contract to drive for Andy Granatelli. He won his first 500 victory by backing off the throttle when his engine began overheating early in the race. He lasted while other leaders faltered.

More often, Andretti charges. He drives on the narrow edge of disaster. "If you start thinking you may get hurt," he says, "you may as well get out of racing." This attitude earned him thirty championship car victories—second only to Foyt's forty-two. But while pushing his racing equipment to the limit, he sometimes breaks it—which is where he was in the middle of May.

Shortly after Mario arrived, his crew pushed the McNamara into the open. One of them rushed to place wooden blocks behind each wheel. A respectful circle of onlookers gathered. "OK, let's crank it," said Vince.

Attracted by the engine sound, Andy Granatelli popped out of the garage. Vince handed him the throttle. Andy signaled one of the other crewmen, who handed him an opened can of STP radiator treatment. Andy slowly poured the milky liquid into the auxiliary radiator behind the driver's seat. It looked almost like a television commercial.

RAMMMMM! Chuckle-chuckle-chuckle. RAMMMMMM! Chuckle-chuckle-chuckle. RAMMMMM! Andy raced the engine. Some of the milky liquid started leaking out of one radiator hose. A crewman moved in to tighten it. Next door, Jerry Karl and his mechanic pushed their car toward the track.

Andy reached forward and flipped the ignition switch. The engine died. The crew started to push the McNamara back into the garage for more adjustments. Later that afternoon Mario would hit 164 miles per hour before a rainstorm ended practice. But at that moment Al Unser came zipping through the garage area driving an electric cart. Joe Leon-ard rode beside him. Unser moved the tiller and the car careened slalom style around the rear of the McNamara.

"Hey, you're going to break another leg," one of the STP crewmen shouted after him. Unser glanced back over his shoulder laughing. So did Leonard. That's the way it had been with the Johnny Lightning team all month. Later that afternoon, Al Unser would turn a practice lap in 170.293 mph.

A few minutes after the STP garage doors closed, Sam Posey passed, carrying a black leather bag containing his helmet. "You ready?" shouted one of the mechanics at the Rockwell machine shop nearby.

"I'm ready," said Sam. Then he noticed the Hawk still parked outside the STP garage. He stopped. He looked at it—almost lovingly—for several seconds. Then he continued toward the track.

Joe Leonard, George Bignotti, and others

At nine o'clock Friday morning, Mark Donohue's blue and gold Sunoco racer sat in the pit ready to run, but the track was wet. Each minute the track remained closed limited the time of those preparing for qualifications the following day. The well-prepared Donohue could afford the delay. But many mechanics and drivers needed every minute's practice they could get.

One of these was Joe Leonard, thirty-five years old from San Jose, California. Because of contract problems, he had not competed since December. His car was new to him. His practice times had lagged three or four miles per hour behind those of his teammate, Al Unser.

He waited in the Johnny Lightning garage, polishing the plastic visor of his helmet with a handkerchief. Two years earlier, Leonard had set a qualifying record with one of Andy Granatelli's turbine cars that still stood. He drove four laps at an average speed of 171.559 miles per hour, with one lap in 171.953. His last warm-up lap had been clocked unofficially in 173.4. Leonard won the pole and led the race until 191 laps: then his fuel pump broke. "The record is something I'm proud of," Leonard said, "but it hasn't meant a thing to me in dollars and cents."

Art Pollard stopped to talk with Leonard. A. J. Foyt wandered over from his garage several doors away. While the three drivers talked, chief mechanic George Bignotti helped change the plugs of Leonard's racer. He paid little attention to the drivers nearby.

For a half dozen years Foyt and Bignotti, driver and mechanic, had come to the Speedway as a team. Two of Foyt's three Indianapolis victories were with Bignotti. Four of Foyt's five national championships were with Bignotti.

George Bignotti became interested in racing through an older brother who owned a race car. After World War II he began building autos. Mostly he raced around San Francisco, but in 1956 Bignotti built an Indianapolis car for one of his drivers—Johnny Boyd. It was smaller and lighter than any other car at the track. Boyd qualified twelfth and within thirty-five laps had moved to fourth. Then the car developed an oil leak. A week later Boyd used the same car to set a track record at Milwaukee.

In 1957, and again in 1959, Boyd and Bignotti got sixth. "I led the race in 1958 and had to change a tire in the last three laps," Bignotti recalled. "That pushed me back to third. Well, that's fate."

In 1960, A. J. Foyt joined the team. Though only twenty-five at the time, Foyt had strong ideas as to how his car should handle. Bignotti proved equally strongminded. "My biggest argument with A. J.," said Bignotti, "was that he wanted to change things without even going out to sit in the car."

At Indianapolis in 1962 a wheel came off Foyt's car and he spun out of the race, which Roger Ward eventually won. Returning to the pits, Foyt snapped: "The only one I can trust to work on my car is my father!"

Bignotti and Foyt split. That year, Ward took away Foyt's national title. "He would outrun me in the straightaways," Ward recalls, "but I would drive all over him in the corners." Bignotti and Foyt patched their quarrel to win two more national titles in 1963 and 1964 and then the 500 in 1964.

Foyt campaigned in a rear-engine Lotus with a Ford engine toward the end of that season. In the month before Indianapolis in 1965, Bignotti completely rebuilt the car. Foyt won the pole.

During the race, Bignotti signaled Foyt to pit for fuel on the sixty-ninth lap, but Foyt kept running. Five laps later his car ran out of gas. "He came in jerking the engine and the gears all the way down the straightaway. He went out and started catching Jimmy Clark, then the rear end popped. I felt we lost the race for no reason at all, so I quit."

In 1966, two Bignotti cars—driven by Jackie Stewart and Graham Hill—were running one-two with ten laps remaining. Stewart lost oil pressure, but Hill coasted home first.

In 1967, Bignotti hired Al Unser, who responded by finishing second, the year of Foyt's third victory. "A. J.'s a great driver," admits Bignotti. "In the last few years he's learned a lot. But I don't think anybody can drive, try to be mechanic, and run the team. Somewhere along the line, he's got to lose something."

Bignotti signaled his crew to push Leonard's car to the track. As he checked the car's tires at the Firestone tire area, the McLaren crew was nearby at Goodyear checking car 73, now the mount of Peter Revson. Revson stood behind the car observing the actions of the crew. Revson's teammate, however, would not be Chris Amon. Amon had left Indianapolis.

At 9:40 a.m. Harlan Fengler climbed into the pace car to tour the track. Two minutes later he returned to announce: "It looks like another fifteen minutes. We've got three wet spots in critical areas."

Joe Leonard sat in a cart behind the pit wall sipping a soft drink. Lee Roy Yarbrough's car 67 appeared. Yarbrough of Columbia, South Carolina, a NASCAR driver, had won seven Super Speedway victories the previous year. The Ford Motor Company named him their driver of the year. His luck at the Speedway, however, had been poor. In 1965, mechanical trouble halted his rookie test. He passed it the following year but made no attempt to qualify. In 1967, Yarbrough wrecked one car in practice, qualified in a second, then crashed during the race. In 1969, he almost missed the start when his engine wouldn't catch.

Up in the stands Rick Muther sat watching. The turbine car was being repaired. On Thursday he had blown the Offy engine of car 38. Al Unser arrived at the track, chatted several minutes with an official, then left for Gasoline Alley. The lights on the scoring pylon flashed: "00:00:00," a test for tomorrow's qualifications. Soon they pushed Al Unser's car into the pits next to Leonard's.

At 10:15 a.m. the green light came on. Leonard climbed out of the cart and into his car. The cars swarmed onto the track like bees heading for honey: Mario Andretti, Mark Donohue, Larry Cannon, Lee Kunzman, Steve Krisiloff, Lee Roy Yarbrough. Lloyd Ruby headed onto the track as Leonard completed his third lap. Krisiloff headed into the pits and after one more lap, so did Leonard. Bignotti had a wide grin on his face. Leonard hopped out of the car. "Boy, it's got it!" he said.

"That's the way it's supposed to work," said Bignotti, rubbing his hands.

They pushed Leonard's car back toward Gasoline Alley as Al Unser arrived, dressed to go racing. Bignotti stood beside another crewman who flashed Al his times as he passed, most of them just under 170 mph. Then Unser returned to the pits. The mechanics buzzed around his car. Climbing out, Al set his helmet in the cockpit and placed his gloves across the front hood. He rubbed his mouth once, then passed his fingers through his hair. He stood a moment gazing at his car in the way an artist regards a fine painting.

During the first half of May, Al Unser consistently ran faster than any other driver at the Speedway. But nothing is certain in racing. That afternoon Johnny Rutherford, down to speeds of 161 on Wednesday, reached 168. Joe Leonard, so happy in the morning, burned a piston in the afternoon. Nobody knew how fast A. J. Foyt might go.

Foyt had a habit of "sandbagging" in practice. He would run hard through three turns, then ease off on the fourth. The next lap he might slow on a different turn. He rarely put four fast turns together to give the other drivers a clue as to what speed might beat him. But that afternoon a race fan sitting on Turn Four clocked Foyt just before he backed off coming into the straightaway. Foyt hit 172.5 mph.

Meanwhile, Andy Granatelli stood behind Mario Andretti's car with a jeweler's glass in one eye. Mario had just run several practice laps, and Andy was examining the plugs. He wanted to check the tune of a new engine the STP crew had installed overnight. If the plug is colored black, it means the engine is running too rich. If the plug is white, the engine is running lean. Andy smiled. The color was a proper shade of cocoa brown.

Mario had crossed the runway to where Lloyd Ruby lay on the grass resting. Mario, who weighs 135 pounds, playfully sat down on Lloyd's hip. The big Texan looked up and smiled. But several hours later Lloyd Ruby would not be smiling. After practice, USAC officials picked the order in which drivers would qualify the following day. Out of forty-three numbers drawn, they picked Lloyd Ruby forty-third.

The first day of qualifications– the battle for the pole

Several thousand people waited in the dark outside the Speedway gates on Saturday morning, the first day of qualifications. When the gate opened, precisely at six, they stampeded. Within minutes, all the front row seats in the upper deck of the grandstand had been claimed, even though the first qualifying run was not due to begin for five hours.

Nearly 200,000 race fans attended the first day of qualifications. Many people consider the battle for the pole more exciting than the 500 race itself.

On the main straightaway, the scoring pylon glowed with the numbers of racing cars in the order in which they would attempt to qualify: 39, 77, 45, 31, 9, 7, 59, 56, 44. Muther, Kunzman, Glotzbach, Malloy, Johncock, Foyt, Ates, Simon topped the list.

Despite having been first on the track when it opened on May 1, Muther owed his position to the luck of the draw. Obtaining a low number was important for two reasons. First, the pole winner is settled the first day. Second-day qualifiers, no matter how fast, would start the 500 race behind the slowest first-day qualifier. Drivers making the race the next weekend (on the third and fourth day of qualifications) would start still further back. The Indianapolis 500 is rarely won by anyone who fails to start in the first three rows.

Another edge goes to the early qualifier. On a sunny day, the track would be cooler and faster at eleven than at midafternoon.

Once thirty-three cars have qualified, the bumping begins. If another driver should qualify at a faster speed, the slowest car of the thirty-three gets dropped. The new qualifier moves into the rear of the field.

George Bignotti's two drivers had drawn numbers in the middle of the qualifying lineup: eleventh for Leonard, twentieth for Al Unser. Bignotti knew the effect that a hot midday sun could have on Al's chances, so when he opened the Johnny Lightning garage shortly after six and saw the dark clouds overhead, he rubbed his hands together and grinned. "Well," he said, "if the weather stays like this, we'll go after them."

On the other end of Gasoline Alley, Rolla Vollstedt's car 21 sat propped up on oil cans, its wheels off. Vollstedt had a different reaction. "I'm praying for rain," he said, then looked up at the clouds overhead and shook his fist: "Come down in buckets!"

A mechanic walking past heard him, turned, and swore.

At nine the track should have opened for practice, but it remained wet. Vince Granatelli and his crew continued to tinker with Mario Andretti's car. They had stayed up all night replacing the engine. Bill Dredge, an STP vice president, arrived carrying a tray of coffee and food and paused to talk with a friend: "I came by here last night at eleven and the engine was lying in pieces all over the floor."

At 9:30 a.m. the sun peeked briefly out of the clouds, then disappeared again. The main straightaway grandstands already were packed with people. Cars jammed the highway surrounding the Speedway for miles in all directions. On the track the only vehicles moving were trucks trying to dry the still damp surface. The race cars were brought out to the pits one by one and parked under plastic tarpaulins. Their drivers stood around and waited.

* * *

Shortly after eleven, Harlan Fengler announced the track was open for practice and the drivers in their cars swarmed from the pit area, all still searching for speed. One found it: Johnny Rutherford ran four practice laps over 170 miles per hour—the best: 170.7. Lloyd Ruby reached 171 mph, then parked his car for the long wait.

Others had less luck. Sonny Ates, driving in car number 59, the Sugarripe Prune Special, came through Turn Three too fast and smashed his car into the concrete wall. "I just lost it," he explained later. "The back end got out on me and away we went." Gary Bettenhausen streaked back to the pits, smoke billowing from the rear of his turbocharger. Jim Hurtubise spun in the second turn and Greg Weld in the third. Neither hit the wall. Joe Leonard burned another piston in his engine.

At 12:25 p.m., Rick Muther sat in the Jack Adams Special number 38 rapidly chewing a piece of gum. The USAC officials in the control tower above waited to record his time.

Harlan Fengler appeared, carrying a rolled-up yellow flag in one hand. Fengler checked his watch, then kneeled to talk to the driver. "You understand now that you can take three warm-up laps," said the chief steward.

Muther nodded.

"When you are ready to begin your qualifying run," Fengler continued, "raise your left hand. Are you wearing the armband?"

Muther raised his hand, exhibiting a bright yellow sleeve attached to his left forearm. Fengler seemed satisfied. He continued: "When you cross the starting line you'll receive the green flag. At the end of the third lap, we'll give you the white flag and on the fourth the checkered flag—unless your crew calls you off. Any questions?"

Muther shook his head. Fengler signaled crew chief Howard Millican to proceed. The car's engine rumbled to life. The waiting crowd responded with a loud cheer. As Muther headed toward the track, Millican and his crew walked the other way, toward the north end of the pits. Millican now had the yellow flag tucked under his arm. His crew would time Muther out of the fourth turn. If his time appeared too slow, a wave of the flag would cancel the attempt. The car could make two more qualifying attempts at a later time.

The night before, Rodger Ward, working as a television interviewer for Station WISH-TV, had questioned a number of drivers about speeds. Most felt that the pole would be won with 171 to 172 mph and that it would take better than 164 mph to make the race.

After three warm-up laps, Muther streaked past, his left hand lifted. Three-and-a-half minutes and ten miles later, he came past on his fourth lap. Howard Millican still had the yellow flag under his arm. Rick Muther became the first driver to qualify for the Indianapolis 500. His average speed: 165.654 mph.

While Rick Muther took one more lap to slow down, Jim Malloy, who had drawn fourth yesterday, pulled from the pits. Two drivers had passed. Neither Lee Kunzman nor Charlie Glotzbach had achieved speeds fast enough to justify an attempt.

Rick Muther drove into an area surrounded by flags and photographers. Track announcer Jim Phillipe pointed a microphone at the driver and asked him if he was satisfied with the time: "Yes sir," Muther answered. "I sure am. We had a long hard week, and I just picked up speed today."

"Any idea where you picked it up?" asked Phillipe.

"In my right foot," Muther replied.

As Millican and the crew pushed the car back to Gasoline Alley, Jim Malloy rushed beneath the flapping checkered flag. Malloy qualified more than two mph faster than Muther. At the end of the day, he would hold the position on the outside of the third row in the starting field. Gordon Johncock started fast, but his lap times began to drop, and he called off his attempt.

Three race fans leaped to their feet cheering and holding a banner overhead, as the orange-colored car number 7 began rolling down the runway. 61-64-67-70 CALLING FOR FOYT, said the banner.

Foyt was predicting that the pole would be won in 174 mph.

As A. J. Foyt rounded Turn Four, moving down into the straightaway, the fans in the grandstand craned their necks for a better look. Starter Pat Vidan stood on the raised platform by the starting line holding the green flag in his hand. "Here he is," said the loudspeaker. "See if he takes it . . ."

Suddenly Foyt's left hand came up and Vidan twisted and twirled the flapping flag like a juggler performing on stage. Foyt moved past him, an orange blur, and the loudspeaker began the drone that accompanied each driver on his qualifying run:

". . .and the green flag is on. A. J. Foyt is into the first turn. Coming off the corner, he's off the short stretch. Moving down into the number two turn now. Off number two and he's in the back stretch...."

A minute later the announcer gave the first lap time: "52.60 seconds. Speed 171.103 for A. J. Foyt! Leaving the short stretch moving into the fourth corner...."

The crowd roared when they heard Foyt's first lap speed. But even as the loudspeaker drone continued, his time began to drop. He came past the starting line the second time having lost three tenths of a second, a drop of one mph on that lap. The speed he lost on that lap would cost A. J. Foyt the pole. His third and fourth laps dropped into the 169-mph bracket. Foyt had a four-lap average of 170.004 mph.

"The wind was pretty bad," Foyt explained several minutes later over the track loudspeaker system. "I got sideways a couple of times and finally decided it just wasn't worth it." Foyt's remarks, however, seemed less directed to the 200,000 fans than to the drivers behind him in line.

Sonny Ates and Jim Hurtubise, two of the early morning spin victims, stood next in line. Ates's car had been demolished. Hurtubise wasn't ready. They passed their chances to qualify. So did Dick Simon, who had gone no faster than 159 mph in practice during the month. Jigger Sirois, as well as Joe Leonard, had damaged his engine that morning. At 1:20 p.m., Bruce Walkup qualified the Wynn's Spitfire 97 in 166.459 mph. Rolla Vollstedt's plea for rain had failed; his driver John Cannon passed.

Then Tony Adamowicz pulled onto the track in the Patrick Petroleum Special number 36. The twenty-nine-year-old bachelor from Torrance, California, had worked at the White House while in the Army. Before Presidential trips, Adamowicz would travel ahead establishing communications. President John F. Kennedy called him by his first name. After Kennedy's assassination, Tony Adamowicz quit the service and became a race driver.

"On the road courses you can make a mistake in one turn and make it up on another," Tony had explained earlier to Indianapolis *News* reporter Dave Overpeck. "Here you bobble just the amount of time it takes you to click a stopwatch on and off and you lose a mile or two an hour. And there's no place to make it up."

As Tony Adamowicz rolled toward Turn One, he experienced a "bobble." It was not his but that of the officials. Though Pat Vidan waved the green flag, the light at the end of the main straightaway changed from green to yellow. Tony Adamowicz, who had reached 166.3 mph on his warm-up lap, released the throttle and glided through the first turn and short chute. Suddenly the green light appeared again.

He kept going, but the "bobble" dropped his first lap time to 160.829 mph. He quickly regained his previous speed, but as Adamowicz came off the fourth turn, crew chief Mike Devin had to decide whether or not to abandon the attempt. Should they protest? They might not get back on the track for another attempt that day. Devin decided that Tony's average speed (164.820 mph) should qualify him for the race. As Tony passed the starting line on his final lap, Devin did not raise the yellow flag.

Carlos Pairetti's car was not ready. George Snider qualified with a time of 167.660 mph in one of A. J. Foyt's cars. "Do you think it would be very fair of you to pass your boss?" Snider was asked. He said yes. He also complained about the wind in Turns Two and Three. Wally Dallenbach passed his attempt.

When Dan Gurney pulled into the pits after recording a speed good enough only for the middle of the fourth row, his crew had long faces. "The power was there," he said, "but I couldn't get through the corners." Gurney's last two laps had dropped to 166 and 164 after opening laps in the 168 range. Sam Posey didn't get that far. His engine exploded after his second lap.

Finally, at 1:57 p.m. Al Unser began his qualifying run, roaring into the first turn hard and fast—almost too fast. "The back end jumped out from underneath me," he would say later, "and I thought I had lost it." Unser found himself too high in the turn. He didn't let up. He stayed on the throttle, figuring that it wouldn't matter whether he hit the wall at 172 or 169 mph.

But the car swung safely through that turn, across the chute, and into the next turn. At the end of lap one Al Unser had a time of 170.358 mph—good, but not as good as Foyt's opener. Unser's second lap bettered that of Foyt's by two-tenths of a second. Parnelli Jones stood next to George Bignotti at the entrance to the pits waving his arms wildly. He wanted his driver to go still faster.

Unser did on lap three, but on Turn Four the rear end of his car started to break loose again. Unser quickly corrected—and his third lap time was identical to that of his first—but he began to worry whether he was charging too hard. On the last circuit he concentrated on driving smoothly—and succeeded. His time dropped below 170 mph. Nevertheless, as he pulled into the pits the crowd applauded the new leader.

Al Unser had beaten Foyt's time—170.221 mph to 170.004 mph. On the clock the margin was less than three-tenths of a second.

Mark Donohue next qualified with 168.911 mph, a speed that would put him in the middle of the second row. When asked if the wind bothered him, he remarked dryly, "That seems to be the common excuse." Steve Krisiloff averaged 162.448 mph, but many rated his time as too slow for him to last. As Johnny Rutherford began his qualifying run in the Patrick Petroleum Special number 18, Al Unser stood being interviewed on television. Suddenly the smile on his face froze. He had heard something on the track loudspeaker. "What was that?" he asked Parnelli Jones.

Parnelli told Al that the loudspeaker had just announced Johnny Rutherford's first lap time as 171.135 mph. "He's got us beat," said Al, no longer smiling.

Parnelli shook his head. "He's got three laps to go."

Johnny Rutherford later described his feelings coming down the main straightaway when he saw his pit crew jumping up and down and waving: "I knew either something was falling off the car or we were going real fast."

On the second lap, however, Rutherford had trouble. "It was just an instant," he would remember. "I was coming out of Turn Four, and I got a little close to the gray outside the groove. I just backed off the throttle for an instant to check my slide. I think it probably cost me the pole."

When Rutherford crossed the finish line, his four-lap time was 3:31:50 (or 170.213 mph). Mike Devin and his crew danced along the infield grass flashing the V for victory sign. But that was before the officials in the control tower compared times. Al Unser had done 3:31:49. Johnny Rutherford thus failed by one-hundredth of a second. The margin of victory for Al Unser in the ten-mile run was two-and-a-half feet.

Rutherford actually had run his last warm-up lap before taking the green flag in 171.4 mph. If he had raised his hand one lap early, he would have won the pole. But Indianapolis is full of ifs.

At the moment of apparent victory for Rutherford, Al Unser, his face as overcast as the sky above, had returned his attention to the television interviewer. He explained how the wind had bothered him. When Rutherford's total time was announced finally on the track loudspeaker,

Unser quickly turned again from the camera to Parnelli Jones: "He didn't beat me?"

"He didn't beat you," said Parnelli, looking as though he might cry.

"Oh, hey!" shouted Al, and he laughed. Then he turned back to the camera. "That's getting too close for comfort."

The television interviewer asked him how he felt sitting on the pole, but Al Unser had retreated again behind the mask of calm that most drivers show to the public. "I'm not there yet," he said.

But there would be no more surprises left for Al Unser that day. Roger McClusky and Art Pollard ran fast enough to flank Mark Donohue in the second row. Bobby Unser and Mario Andretti qualified inside Jim Malloy on the third row. "It's a relief just to be in the field," said Mario, "but frankly, I'm a little disappointed."

At 3:42 p.m. Harlan Fengler stood before the nose of Gary Bettenhausen's car, ready to signal him onto the track, when the rain began to fall. It drizzled, then rained harder, then stopped. Trucks ran over the track trying to dry it; then the rain began anew. Waiting in line when Fengler officially closed the track at 6:15 p.m. was the man who had run three 171 mph laps that morning in practice: Lloyd Ruby.

Top three qualifier–and others

The sun shone brightly early Sunday morning. At 8:30 a.m. the cars of the three top qualifiers were parked on the main straightaway. Behind them stood drivers Al Unser, Johnny Rutherford, and A. J. Foyt.

Several dozen photographers were taking pictures. One of the cameramen suggested that the drivers climb into their cars, but A. J. Foyt—wearing white slacks and a blue striped sweater—firmly shook his head. He didn't want to dirty his slacks.

"A. J. is kind of bully-like," commented one of several guards who had stopped to watch.

"Yeah, just the way old Vukovich was," said another.

Two hours later the track filled with speeding race cars and their drivers: Peter Revson, Donnie Allison, Carl Williams (who learned only that morning that Amon's car number 75 was now his), Mel Kenyon, Gary Bettenhausen. Although he had qualified the day before, Lee Roy Yarbrough took several practice laps. So did Mark Donohue.

Lloyd Ruby appeared in car number 12 and began turning laps over 167 miles per hour. Then suddenly a puff of white smoke erupted from his engine. Ruby had burned a piston. The engine would have to be rebuilt. Ruby's crew pushed his car back to the garage and began to ready his other car, number 25. He had not sat in 25 for five days.

Meanwhile Peter Revson, who had sat waiting in line when yesterday's rain fell, hit 169.2 in a practice lap. And after sixteen days of nervous waiting, George Follmer climbed into the cockpit of Andretti's old Hawk.

The track closed for ceremonies and Al Unser received a $6,000 check from Sprite as part of his prize as fastest qualifier. The pole was worth $19,200 to the Johnny Lightning team, including a $5,000 award for chief mechanic George Bignotti.

At noon the track opened again. Gary Bettenhausen and Peter Revson quickly qualified for the race. Revson's speed of 167.942 mph would have placed him in the fourth row ahead of Dan Gurney had he had the opportunity to run on Saturday. Qualifying on Sunday, however, he had to settle for the outside of row six.

Ronnie Bucknum went two laps better than 164 mph; then his crew raised the yellow flag calling him off. He had been moving faster than two already qualified drivers, Tony Adamowicz and Steve Krisiloff. Some railbirds felt Krisiloff's time of 162.448 mph might prove fast enough. Bucknum's crew obviously didn't agree.

Even while Bucknum coasted down the backstretch, the track guards sounded their whistles and a red, white, and blue star-spangled car began moving down the runway. "And now Lloyd Ruby," said track announcer Tom Carnegie.

On his final warm-up lap, Lloyd Ruby came rolling out of the fourth turn hard and fast and down the groove, but the flag did not wave. "Lloyd Ruby did not pick up the flag," announced Carnegie. "Apparently he was not happy with the speeds he was getting in the practice laps."

But Lloyd Ruby *was* happy with his speed. He had hit 168 mph on his third lap. Coming down the straightaway, Lloyd had raised his left hand to signal the starter. Vidan missed the signal. Ruby wasn't wearing the yellow band on his forearm. "It flaps around too much in the breeze," Ruby had said when he refused it.

Ruby pulled into the pits, his engine running, and asked Harlan Fengler why the flag hadn't dropped. When told, he asked for another chance. Fengler agreed and Lloyd Ruby roared back onto the track. This time when his hand raised, the green flag waved.

When his first lap time of 168.982 mph was announced, the crowd broke into applause. At the announcement of his second lap in 169.428

mph, there were screams of joy. Ruby roared by on his third lap and through Turns One and Two. Announcer Tom Carnegie began: "The time on that third lap is—"

Suddenly a puff of smoke erupted from the rear of Ruby's racer. "There goes the engine on that car!" interrupted the other announcer, Chuck Bailey.

The crowd moaned in disappointment. "Another bad break for Lloyd Ruby," said Carnegie. The third lap speed had been 168.729 mph, before Ruby had burned another piston. He had been asked to run one lap too many.

Wally Dallenbach, who had made no attempt on Saturday because of engine trouble, qualified in 165.601 mph in one Sprite special, then was followed to the line by Mel Kenyon in another. Kenyon, thirty-seven years old, first tried the Speedway in 1965 but was bumped from the field. Later that year he crashed in a championship race at Langhorne, Pennsylvania, severely burning himself. He lost half his left hand.

He arrived at the Speedway the following year with a leather glove on that hand featuring a socket built into the palm. The socket fitted over a knob on his steering wheel, permitting him to drive. In four years he never qualified higher than fourteenth, but placed fifth, sixteenth, third, and fourth and completed 775 out of a possible 800 laps—more than any other driver during this span.

Although Mel and his brother Don Kenyon built midget autos for other drivers in nearby Lebanon, Indiana, he came to the track this year with a Coyote purchased from A. J. Foyt. Foyt ran Ford engines in his Coyotes; Kenyon decided to use an Offenhauser. This caused venting problems: the engine would go three fast laps, then begin to sputter. During Saturday's qualifications, Kenyon ran two laps just under 169 mph before his engine quit. Foyt came to the Sprite garage that night and suggested corrections. On Sunday Kenyon qualified into the eighth row with 165.906 mph but didn't seem happy. "We had a chance yesterday for the second row," he said. "It would have been nice to get up out of the sand."

Carl Williams qualified in Chris Amon's former car with 166.590 mph. Then at 1:12 p.m. for the first time since the trials began, no more drivers waited in line.

"The track is now open for practice," announced Harlan Fengler. Soon a half dozen cars had moved onto the pavement: Billy Vukovich, Greg Weld, Carlos Pairetti, Jim Hurtubise, Jimmy McElreath, Kevin Bartlett. George Follmer took his first practice lap in the Hawk. Mario Andretti stood nearby offering advice. Back in the Ruby garage, the mechanics worked frantically pulling the engine from his car.

Later in the afternoon Kevin Bartlett tried qualifying but couldn't get car 74 moving even over 160 mph. His crew called off the attempt. Bartlett then climbed into 77, Revson's former car. Charlie Glotzbach held a stopwatch while Al Miller practiced in the car originally assigned to him.

At 4:30 p.m. Veith crashed. He was unhurt, but the track closed while workers swept away the debris. Lloyd Ruby meanwhile stood in the shadow of the scoring pylon. The pylon contained the number of twenty-three qualified cars. Ten spaces remained vacant.

Ruby's car containing a newly installed engine had just been pushed onto the track. He frowned because the yellow light meant he must wait. He walked over to the pit wall and sat down.

"Hey, Lloyd," a boy with a camera around his neck called to him.

Lloyd Ruby turned. His first impulse was to rise and pose for a picture. Then he remembered what was happening. "Not now," he said almost gently. "Wait until I come in. I'm—" His voice drifted off. He shook his head and turned back to the track.

Two of Ruby's mechanics sat on the pavement leaning against their racing car's wide wheels. Crew chief Dave Laycock stood on the runway looking north. "Rube," he said, "looks like they're pushing some cars to the line right now."

Ruby turned his head to the right but said nothing.

"I think Johncock is up there," said Laycock. "I'll go check." He ran down toward the tower but returned a few minutes later to report it was a false alarm.

Ruby gazed to the left down the straightaway at the still yellow light. "That light!" he muttered. "Come on!"

When the green light flashed shortly before five, Lloyd Ruby moved quickly into his car and rolled out onto the track. He did several laps, one of them in 165.4. He returned to the pits and conferred with

Dave Laycock. The other members of the crew tensely watched. "Let's go," said Lloyd Ruby finally.

The crew pushed the car south and parked it before the tower. It seemed as though the other drivers had been waiting politely for Lloyd Ruby to take the lead. A. J. Foyt directed his crew to slide Donnie Allison's car into line. Joe Leonard moved in behind him. In less than a minute, seven cars stood waiting to qualify.

Harlan Fengler leaned over Lloyd Ruby sitting in the cockpit of his star-spangled car. "Whenever you're ready," Fengler said. Ruby began rolling down the runway. Thin smoke clouds trailed behind him.

Ruby took only one warm-up lap, then raised his hand immediately for the flag. He was wearing the yellow armband. Lloyd Ruby's first lap was slow—165.8 mph—then, coming out of Turn Three: another puff of smoke.

A. J. Foyt, waiting in the pits to help Donnie Allison, jumped onto the pit wall and craned his neck, trying to see down the straightaway. One of the pit guards told him to get down. A. J. ignored the guard. Ruby came rolling around Turn Four, his engine shut off. He coasted through the pits heading straight for Gasoline Alley. He turned straight in and disappeared from sight. His crew walked slowly along the infield grass. They would face a long week of waiting. Foyt stepped down off the wall, shaking his head.

Allison qualified. Then Leonard. Then Johncock. Bentley Warren failed. George Follmer qualified after only twenty practice laps that day in the Hawk. Ronnie Bucknum took two laps, then came in. With time getting short, Kevin Bartlett pulled his car out of line to give other faster drivers a chance. Sam Posey moved his car to the end of the line. He didn't want to make a try that day; he wanted to be standing in line at six, which would give him an early starting position the next week. Bentley Warren tried again, failed again. Jim Hurtubise backed off on the fourth lap of his attempt when he could go no faster than 164 mph.

At 5:58 p.m. Rolla Vollstedt's crew pushed John Cannon in car number 17 to the line. One of the crewmen stuck a starter motor into the rear of the car. The starter spun the engine, which failed to catch. They tried again. The engine caught, then died. Vollstedt looked anxiously at his mechanic: "Once more, Hal." Once more and it died again. The next driver in line was Bentley Warren, ready for his third and final attempt. Behind him waited Dick Simon, Jim Hurtubise, Al Miller, Darrel Dockery, and Sam Posey.

Up in the control tower a hand holding a pistol appeared out of a corner window. At precisely six o'clock, the pistol fired, and qualifications ended until the next week.

As Bolla Vollstedt's crew pushed their still unstarted car back toward Gasoline Alley, one of Bentley Warren's mechanics smiled at Harlan Fengler: "They sure hung in there, didn't they?"

Some more tries–and two shoestrings

With the first weekend of trials past, Gasoline Alley now divided into two groups. The first group consisted of those unqualified. They continued to work, but with increased tension. Only five more days of practice remained for them to find the right combination of car and driver—or wait until next year.

The second group consisted of those already qualified. They were easy to spot at the Speedway on Monday morning: they were the ones smiling.

Gary Bettenhausen climbed into his backup car number 78 to shake it down so Larry Dickson later might attempt to qualify it. A. J. Foyt returned to Houston to tend his engine business. Al Unser did several laps in his Johnny Lightning Special, the fastest being 169.619 miles per hour. George Bignotti then told Al's crew to push the car back to the garage so the engine could be rebuilt.

Shortly after one in the afternoon, mechanic Grant King and his crew pushed the Art Pollard Car Wash Special number 10 to the Firestone garage for a tire check, then out to the pits. Pollard, following behind him, was surrounded by autograph seekers.

Forty-three years old and a grandfather, Art Pollard was the oldest driver already qualified for the 500. Pollard asked his mechanic if they had filled the tanks and, when King said yes, Pollard squeezed his 200 pounds into the car. Most drivers practice and qualify at Indianapolis with their fuel tanks only partly filled. This not only reduces the fire danger but allows them to go fast. Seventy-five gallons of methanol add 525 pounds weight to a car. Since he would be starting the race with tanks full, Pollard wanted to see how the car would handle.

After Pollard completed several practice runs, Grant King reached into the toolbox for a piece of yellow chalk and marked each of the car's four tires: "Race Set #1." Then Pollard climbed out and helped his crew push the car back to Gasoline Alley.

Art Pollard's car had been running smoothly all month and he looked like a possible winner. One other qualified driver working on the engine of his car that day did little talking about winning. Steve Krisiloff admitted that with a qualifying average of only 162.448 mph, he probably would get bumped from the field. "I'm praying for rain next weekend," he said.

Krisiloff, at age twenty-three, ranked as the youngest driver at the Speedway and also the one with the smallest racing budget. *Indianapolis Star* sports editor Bob Collins wrote of Krisiloff: "He never has to worry about people roaming into his garage and stealing spare parts—they are all under the hood of his car." Krisiloff functioned as the chief and only mechanic for his car, except on weekends when his father would arrive from their home in Parsippany, New Jersey (just outside New York City).

Of the twenty-seven drivers already qualified, only Krisiloff had a normally aspirated (or unblown) engine. The rest used turbocharged engines. Krisiloff accepted a green flag on Saturday despite marginal speed, because he couldn't see where he could pick up any more speed at any other time. He didn't use a turbocharged engine because he couldn't afford one.

The turbocharger uses a blower to force air into the engine cylinder. This adds roughly one hundred horsepower to the engine. There was no way in which Steve Krisiloff could win the 500 race in his unblown engine. He knew it, but high places at Indianapolis often go to drivers who merely survive—so he prayed for rain.

Steve Krisiloff didn't suffer the indignity of an empty pocketbook alone. Al Loquasto had named his car the Indy on a Shoestring Special. A film crew trailed him to make a movie on his attempt to qualify for the race. This provided him with enough money for a turbo-Offy. Loquasto looked like a possible qualifier.

Ten minutes before the track closed, Al Blanchard, the STP camera-man, stood on the green of the fifteenth hole of the Speedway golf course outside the track. "I heard this terrible noise," Blanchard said afterward. "It sounded like two biscuits hitting the wall. Then there was a sort of little tinkle as pieces started falling onto the track."

The pieces were parts of Al Loquasto's racing machine. As he came into that turn, his throttle had stuck. He reached for the ignition switch to shut down the engine, but it was too late. He hit the turn too fast and slammed into the wall. The shoestring broke. Loquasto was shaken but unhurt.

As for Blanchard, he said: "It ruined my golf game for the rest of the day."

Simpson on fire and a case of oversteer

Shortly before 10:30 on Tuesday morning, many at the Speedway began to drift north toward the number one turn. Bill Simpson planned to set himself on fire.

Simpson sat down in a chair and watched racing fuel being poured over the legs of his driving suit. The stunt would demonstrate a new fireproof fiber called Kynol. "Down in front!" shouted someone in the crowd, as driver George Snider lit Simpson with a match.

Flames leaped from Simpson's legs. He let the fire burn for thirty-two seconds, then waved to two firemen who sprayed him with foam. Simpson rose undamaged. The crowd returned to the business at hand.

Those who had qualified the previous weekend continued to practice: Lee Roy Yarbrough, Mario Andretti, and Dan Gurney. The blond Gurney sat in the cockpit of his new Eagle, hands folded, the features of his chiseled face immobile, and watched as one of his mechanics dabbed droplets of oil in several spots along the front hood. The oil was to test the air flow.

Gurney ran several laps, the fastest in 168.8 miles per hour, and returned to the pits. Gurney talked with crew chief Wayne Leary. They looked at a notebook. Leary pointed to the oil streaking the back fin. Gurney looked worried, so everyone else looked worried.

Mario Andretti meanwhile was traveling fast. He rushed around the track in 168.5 mph, cutting down low to pass Dick Simon on the inside as he did so. (The other driver had been traveling seven or eight mph slower than Mario at the time.) Simon, in his purple-colored car 44, headed for the pits on the next lap. His brakes squeaked loudly as he halted.

Simon removed his helmet, revealing an almost total lack of hair. He looked up at his mechanic, Phil Wieder. "The back end feels like it's on ice," Simon said. "It just rolls, and as soon as it rolls—*whoosh!*"

Phil nodded and with his wrench made several quick adjustments to the rear end. The driver headed out onto the track once more. Dick Simon, a thirty-six-year-old rookie, had seven children at home in Salt Lake City, Utah, where he headed a life insurance company. Simon had attended the University of Utah on a ski scholarship but broke his ankle while trying to make the US Olympic ski jumping team in 1960.

He became a skydiver, leaping 651 times from an airplane, and won the national parachuting championships in 1965. The following year, high winds collapsed his chute a hundred feet above the ground, and he broke his back in two places. Now he was driving race cars.

Simon never had seen the Speedway until Rolla Vollstedt brought him to Indianapolis the previous winter and drove him around the track. Four inches of snow covered the ground at the time.

After two laps, Simon returned to the pits. "Better?" Phil asked him.

"Not much," the driver replied. "I can make the front push if I do it on purpose, but the back is still loose. It's a bit frightening out there."

"Just be patient," said Phil.

"I'll be patient," Simon said. "But this sweat on my forehead isn't from the heat."

"Push" is a term used by drivers to describe what happens when a car understeers. Push is the opposite of pinch; understeer is the opposite of oversteer. When a car oversteers, it turns too quickly to the left—or pinches—and the back end slides around to the right. As the car slides sideways through the turn, it scrubs the tires, raising their temperatures. The tires may need changing sooner. This sliding also slows the car.

With understeer, however, the driver can use his throttle to help him steer. As he turns the wheel, the front end shifts left. As he applies the throttle, the rear end counters to the right. The tires will run straight through the corner and not overheat. The car then can swing high up near the wall on the short chute at maximum speed. And since the engine revolutions remain high, the engine will have more pickup when the car comes through the next turn and into the straightaway. Of course, too much push or understeer and the driver will have to brake or bury his nose in the wall. So, the mechanics at Indianapolis tinker with their chassis, seeking the proper balance going through the turns.

Simon went back on the track but three laps later returned to the pits. "Worse," he said. "I had no push whatsoever."

Phil looked glumly at his driver.

Later that afternoon Billy Vukovich walked along the fence, accompanied by Gary Bettenhausen and Gary's younger brother, Merle. Merle Bettenhausen ranked sixth in the USAC midget auto standings the previous year and had raced that weekend at a nearby track. A girl standing behind the fence called to him: "Merle, how did you do Sunday?"

"OK for a while," Merle told her.

"Awful," corrected Billy.

Merle glared at Billy: "I said, 'for a while.'"

Awful also described Billy Vukovich's mood. Unable to move faster than 161 mph, he finally had asked Gary Bettenhausen to test his car. Gary agreed, even though his father had died doing a similar favor for a friend.

Billy helped Gary into the car. But Bettenhausen stood three inches shorter than Vukovich, and he had to climb out while they adjusted the seat.

Gary drove the car several laps, then returned to the pits. "No wonder you can't go fast," he shouted, still sitting in the cockpit. "When you back off the throttle, it goes like this." He made a sweeping motion with his hand.

"Take your helmet off," said mechanic Leonard Faas. "I can't hear you."

Bettenhausen climbed out of the cockpit. "When you get on the throttle hard, it comes out, but you can't get on it hard enough."

Vukovich turned to his mechanic. "We can still go in on the shock." He said it almost as though it were a question.

Faas shook his head. "Just turn it. You'll see it won't go any farther."

Gary Bettenhausen said: "Every time you get a little wiggle with the car and you correct it, you make it worse. It's oversteering."

Billy Vukovich simply frowned.

Last minute tries; Jack Brabham makes it

On the twentieth day, the month at Indianapolis ended for Larry Cannon[4*] of Danville, Illinois. He lost control at 145 miles per hour in Turn Three while taking his rookie test. Cannon's car spun and slid 620 feet, then bounced three times against the wall—*boom, boom, boom*!

Cannon's crew might have repaired his car by the weekend, but he wouldn't have time to complete his test. The tests ended officially at six with twenty rookies qualified. Jerry Karl also failed to complete his test. Bill Puterbaugh qualified the very last day.

But while the month ended for Larry Cannon, it had just begun for another driver, Jack Brabham. The three-time world champion had planned to come to Indianapolis much sooner with two cars built in England. A truck strike, however, delayed his plans. The cars finally arrived in town on Sunday, too late to qualify.

Now on Wednesday Brabham stood by the side of a bluish-green racer, numbered 32, the only one of the two he had time to assemble. He squinted up at the midday sun. The track temperature would reach 135 degrees that day, but Jack Brabham had little time to spare.

John Arthur Brabham, born in Sydney, Australia, in 1926, served in the Royal Australian Air Force during World War II. He began racing after the war and in 1955 traveled to Europe to try Grand Prix racing.

[4*] No relation of Canadian John Cannon.

In 1959, and again in 1960, he won the world championships and became the first driver to appear at Indianapolis in a rear-engine car.

In 1962, Brabham began building his own cars, and for three years Dan Gurney drove for him. Often Brabham sat on the sidelines while Gurney raced. Reporters began to ask if he planned to retire. At the Dutch Grand Prix in 1966, a man with a long beard used a cane to hobble out onto the racetrack. The man threw down the cane, removed the beard, and climbed into a racing car. It was Jack Brabham thumbing his nose at reporters who had dubbed him, at age forty, the grand old man of racing. He won that race and, later that year, his third world title. At Indianapolis in 1964 and 1969, he failed to finish.

In June 1969, Brabham's brakes failed in tests at Silverstone, England, and he collided with an earth bank. Nobody observed the accident and Brabham found himself trapped in the car with fuel seeping into the cockpit. He switched off the ignition, turned on the fire extinguisher, then waited for another test driver to pass and discover him. A half hour passed before he was freed. A three-inch steel pin was needed to repair his smashed ankle.

On May 10, 1970, Brabham had appeared at the Monaco Grand Prix, along with Denis Hulme, Chris Amon, and Bruce McLaren. Jackie Stewart surged to an early lead, then dropped out. McLaren also had to stop. Brabham assumed the lead in the twenty-seventh lap of the eighty-lap race. Chris Amon made a run at him, then fell back.

With ten laps remaining, Brabham led by fourteen seconds over Jochen Rindt of Austria. Then Rindt began a charge that brought him within one-and-a-half seconds of the leader starting the last lap. Coming into the final hairpin turn, Brabham saw two slower cars ahead of him. The man who some called Mr. Icewater panicked and passed his braking point. When he did hit the brakes, they locked. He slid into a bale of hay. Rindt swept past him on the inside to win the race, having covered the final lap in record time.

Brabham got his car moving soon enough to finish second, while Denis Hulme placed fourth. "It was one of the biggest disappointments of my life," Brabham said afterward, even though his second place allowed him to hold his championship point lead.[5]

---

[5] Later in the season, Rindt would crash and die in another Grand Prix race.

But now, on Wednesday morning, Jack Brabham had no reason to look in his rear vision mirror. He moved up into the groove and hit 161.2 mph. Later that afternoon, Brabham pushed the speed of his car to near 165 mph. Just before the track closed at six, he sat in his racer, goggles down around his neck, and pressed an index finger against the bridge of his nose. Finally, he climbed out smiling. "We'll be ready to qualify Saturday," said the grand old man of racing.

Jigger Sirois and The City of Memphis Special

Jigger Sirois sat in the cockpit of The City of Memphis Special, watching the dials as the turbine engine wound up behind him, convinced that he would see this year's Indianapolis 500 only from the grandstands.

Earlier that morning mechanic Howard Millican had added a water alcohol injector to the turbine. The car's speed jumped to 163 miles per hour. But under USAC rules, the injector was illegal. Millican knew that. He just wanted to test the car's potential. When he removed the injector, speeds fell by three mph.

Making the race was important to Jigger Sirois for several reasons. The first was money. As a construction worker in Hammond, Indiana, he could have earned $1,500 during May. Instead, Jigger had agreed to drive at the Speedway for 50 percent of whatever prize money he earned. Fifty percent of nothing is nothing.

Second, Jigger hoped to prove his abilities. He wanted to drive regularly on the championship trail, the major leagues of auto racing.

But perhaps the most important reason was pride. Jigger Sirois was tired of being reminded how he could have won the pole last year. The auto writers even had named an award after him: the Jigger Sirois trophy, awarded to the hard-luck racer of the month. He wanted to be remembered for something else.

Jigger had contacted Jack Adams in January, asking for a ride. Adams had three cars: the turbine and two normal racers. Adams also had another driver, Rick Muther. Jigger wanted the turbine, but Muther had first choice.

Adams had entered the turbine car at the Speedway the previous May. But after Andy Granatelli's two near victories with turbine cars, USAC officials had passed rules to cut the air intake on such cars to less than twelve square inches. With that handicap, the 1969 model ran only 158 mph, too slow to qualify.

Over the winter, mechanic Howard Millican built a new lightweight chassis for the same turbine engine. Millican had grown up in Albuquerque, New Mexico, where he knew Bobby Unser. He helped Bobby with his Pikes Peak cars and first came to the Speedway with him in 1964. In 1967 and 1968, he worked for Dan Gurney on the cars of Jochen Rindt, then joined Jack Adams.

He prepared the car in which Jimmy McElreath qualified seventh for the 500 in 1969. "We went about a third of the way and scattered an engine," Howard recalled.

In designing his 1970 turbine car, Howard Millican hoped that its light weight and good handling would overcome the handicap of low horsepower. But his design depended upon obtaining smaller tires. Early in May, he discovered the tire companies couldn't, or wouldn't, provide them.

When it became obvious the turbine wasn't fast enough, Rick Muther switched to the Offy-powered Brabham car 38, in which he qualified on Saturday. Jigger took the 72 car, a Lola, then burned a piston in practice that same day. While the Lola's engine was being repaired, Jack Adams asked Jigger Sirois to help them test the turbine. This meant Jigger would have to go from one car to another and back to the first, which would complicate his qualifying problems. As a Speedway rookie, Jigger knew neither championship cars nor the track very well. "They were such nice people, I didn't want to say no," he said.

The turbine now screamed at high pitch. Howard Millican tapped Jigger twice on the helmet. The car plunged toward the track. Heat waves danced off the pavement behind it. Millican went to stand near the scoring pylon, stopwatch in hand.

Each time one of his cars took the track, Millican had times recorded in four different places. One timer checked each lap. A second timer checked the car's speed on Turn One by clocking it between two marks on the wall. A third timer at the south end of the track clocked the car moving through Turns Three and Four. The final timer obtained the car's straightaway speed from the moment it came off the turn to where it crossed in front of the tower. This enabled Howard to discover what effect different engineering changes had on the car at different parts of the track.

One innovation was to use fourteen-inch-wide tires on the right side compared to ten-inch-wide tires on the left. The left tires also were of smaller diameter. The theory was that the larger outside tires were needed during the constant left turns. The smaller inside tires, however, caused less air drag down the straightaway.

In clocking all cars, Millican discovered that the turbine rated very fast on the turns. He clocked Jigger in Turn One at 5.60 seconds. In comparison, only A. J. Foyt, with 5.55, had a better cornering speed. Mario Andretti and Gordon Johncock clocked 5.65 seconds.

The turbine's basic problem was that it ran down the straightaway only five mph faster than on the corners. "Part of our fast corner speeds," admitted Millican, "is that when you don't go into the corner hard, your chassis doesn't get upset."

In its qualifying setup, a turbo-Ford develops 800 hp and a turbo-Offy develops 750 hp. This permits the fastest drivers to reach 210 to 215 mph straightaway speeds. In comparison, the turbine developed 400 hp (or 420 hp with the illegal injector). Even the unblown engines developed much more power than that.

Howard Millican's stopwatch dangled from the string around his neck as he walked back across the runway. He showed Jigger the clipboard listing his times. Sirois had one lap at 161.5 mph, fastest for the month. But that same day Jack Brabham reached 166.175 mph; Kevin Bartlett did 165.746. Millican calculated that to improve their speed by four mph, they would need an extra seventy-five hp. There was no way he could get it.

Howard Millican followed his crew as they pushed The City of Memphis Special back toward Gasoline Alley. Jigger Sirois went inside the garage to change out of his driver's uniform. The door shut. Then Howard turned to walk toward his other garage and work on the car Rick Muther had qualified for the race. "Well, I guess I've spent enough time fighting windmills for today," he said.

MAY 22, FRIDAY

What speed for the 500?

On the final day before the final weekend of qualifications, Dick Simon found himself. He had been fumbling under 160 miles per hour for most of the month. On Friday his speed jumped to 166.420 mph. He now seemed certain to make the race.

Simon improved by changing his brand of tires from Goodyear to Firestone. The quality of the tires made little difference; the willingness of the tire company to provide assistance did. Of the twenty-seven drivers already qualified, twenty drove on Goodyear tires. Seven used Firestone. When Simon switched brands, Firestone assigned two tire engineers to work full-time with his crew providing temperature readings.

The Firestone engineers discovered that the chassis of Simon's car was bottoming out. "We never realized this," explained Simon, "because it only was happening in the turns under extreme pressure. We corrected the problem by installing heavier springs. Our speeds started to move up quickly."

That afternoon Rodger Ward roamed the Speedway asking different drivers what speed they thought would qualify them for the 500. John Cannon said 165 mph, although he hadn't approached that speed yet. Jigger Sirois anticipated 164. Sam Posey expected the high 164s. Bud Tingelstad said he would accept a high 163. Lloyd Ruby figured on going 166 mph, but he worried about his luck. That afternoon he had to be towed back to his pits after burning the pinion gear in the rear end of car 12. "I'd go fishing this month," he said wryly, "but I probably wouldn't catch any fish." Kevin Bartlett hoped to make the field with 165.5 mph.

Ward also interviewed Jim Hurtubise. "I turned down one hundred sixty-four last week," Hurtubise commented, "and I think it's going to take at least one hundred sixty-five. The car feels ready, and I'm ready. I know I can run over one hundred sixty-five."

Few others shared his optimism. Hurtubise remained a link to another era. He was the only driver of a front-engine car.

Jim Hurtubise first arrived at Indianapolis in 1960. On the second weekend of qualifications, he broke the existing one lap and four lap records by more than two miles per hour. He failed to finish the race because of a broken connecting rod but still was named Rookie of the Year.

In four more years at the Speedway, he placed no higher than thirteenth. At Milwaukee the week after the 1964 race, Hurtubise dueled Rodger Ward and A. J. Foyt for the lead in a 150-mile race. Suddenly Ward skidded coming out of a turn. Foyt swerved to miss him. Hurtubise slammed into Foyt, bounced against the outside wall, and spun along the main straightaway in flames. The impact with the wall knocked Hurtubise unconscious. When firemen extinguished the fire and lifted the driver out of his cockpit, he had burns on 40 percent of his body. It took eight months of treatment before he recovered, and he had little movement in his maimed hands. "Fix them so they can grip a steering wheel," he told the doctors. "It's what I do for a living."

In 1965, Hurtubise returned to racing and placed fourth in USAC's stock car driving standings. He lasted only one lap in the 500 that year and the following May placed twenty-second in a rear-engine car. In 1967, Hurtubise built a pair of front-engine roadsters, the last of the breed. But in three years he qualified only once for the 500: in 1968 when he completed nine laps.

On Friday, Sonny Ates climbed into his backup car and drove several shakedown laps just under 160 mph. After Ates had crashed his first car last Saturday, his crew had labored all week preparing the second one. The memory of his previous crash still haunted him. He had driven very few laps in practice during the month, and he began to consider surrendering his car to a more experienced driver.

Car owner Joe Hunt, meanwhile, searched for a driver capable of qualifying his car 99. Lee Kunzman had practiced in the car all month with little success. Hunt tried Steve Krisiloff, then approached Al Loquasto. Loquasto soon had the car moving near 160 mph. That speed still wouldn't make the race, but at least it gave Loquasto something to do over the weekend.

Later that evening, Loquasto was approached by Paul Brooks, owner of car 35, which Bud Tingelstad had been driving during the month. Tingelstad had reached only 162 mph in it. Brooks wanted Loquasto to attempt to qualify the car. Loquasto weighed the two offers and decided that Brooks's car had the best chance of making the race. He called Joe Hunt and asked if he objected to his switching cars. Hunt said no. Al Loquasto later would regret that call.

Lloyd Ruby's luck changes; three more join the field; three are bumped

Saturday dawned cool and muggy. Six places remained open in the thirty-three-man starting field. During the week a dozen drivers had bettered the 162.448 speed of Steve Krisiloff, the slowest qualifier. Billy Vukovich was not one of them.

A dozen mechanics gathered around his racer during the early practice period. He had just completed several laps in the 162-miles per hour range. One mechanic jacked up the rear end. Crew chief Leonard Faas reached under with a wrench to adjust one of the stabilizer bars. Vukovich climbed back into the car. They started the engine and pushed him back out again, his gears grinding.

One of Vukovich's friends stood behind the pit wall. "What's the reading?" he asked a mechanic.

"No push," was the answer.

The friend nodded.

"He's getting up enough speed to get him all excited again," explained the mechanic. "Not good enough to make the race, but not bad enough to quit."

Vukovich roared past two laps later, and the friend sitting on a tractor checked his stopwatch. It showed Vukovich had done 161.2. "That's not going to do him any good," he frowned.

As several of the drivers pressed to reach race speeds, they made mistakes. Kevin Bartlett almost lost his car on Turn Two before regaining control. Later, at the other end of the track, Sam Posey spun twice without hitting the wall. By 10:30 a.m., the early morning clouds drifted away, leaving the sun shining brightly in the sky.

Lloyd Ruby roared down the main straightaway, in car number 25. He had just turned a lap in 167.3 mph. Only a half dozen car lengths in front of him went Al Loquasto, driving car number 35. Although Loquasto had first sat in the car only that morning, he already reached 164.8 mph. Loquasto, realizing how close he was to his dream of making the race, drove a little deeper into Turn One before letting up on the throttle.

Lloyd Ruby saw Loquasto suddenly spin before him. "Here we go again," Lloyd told himself. He aimed directly at Loquasto's car, figuring that by the time he reached that spot the other driver would be somewhere else. The veteran was right. Loquasto spun upward through the gray stuff to collide with the wall. Ruby zipped past.

He later estimated that he had come within eight inches of hitting Loquasto's spinning car. "I finally found some luck." That afternoon Lloyd Ruby qualified his car so effortlessly that one wondered what all the fuss had been about the previous weekend. He turned three laps over 169 mph, then nervously eased through his fourth lap slower, for an average speed of 168.895 mph. Ruby's time should have given him a starting position in the second row; instead, he would start from row nine.

Lloyd Ruby became the thirty-second qualifier. Before his attempt, Bentley Warren, Sam Sessions, Ronnie Bucknum, and Greg Weld qualified. Kevin Bartlett then hit 165.259 to fill the thirty-third position on the scoring pylon.

The bumping now began. "Steve Krisiloff is sitting on the bubble," announced Tom Carnegie. Krisiloff lost his place when Jerry Grant in car 89 averaged four laps in 165.983 mph. Grant didn't take Krisiloff's place in the sixth row, however. Because he had qualified on the third day, he moved into row ten. But Peter Revson and the other second-day qualifiers moved up one notch.

By six, three more drivers joined the field: Dick Simon, Jack Brabham, and Billy Vukovich. Two hours earlier, Vuky finally had abandoned his first car to climb into the cockpit of the Sugarripe Prune Special number 58, originally brought to the track by Sonny Ates. After only twenty laps of practice, he had his new car moving at 166 mph.

"How many laps did you have in that other car?" a television reporter asked him.

"It felt like forty thousand," Vukovich replied.

Three more drivers thus had been bumped from the field: Tony Adamowicz, Bentley Warren, and Jimmy McElreath. After the track closed, McElreath went wandering through Gasoline Alley hoping to find another ride. He soon found himself standing in front of the garage of A. J. Foyt.

Last day–last chance

"Hey, get your good linen racing flags here!" shouted a vendor outside the Speedway main entrance on Sunday morning. "They're made of silk."

The sun in the sky above was hot, and it would get hotter. Inside the Speedway, several already qualified drivers—including Al Unser and Johnny Rutherford—did some last-minute testing. So did the other front-row driver, A. J. Foyt, but not in the cockpit of his qualified car.

When Jimmy McElreath had stopped by the Foyt garage after qualifications on Saturday, he asked A. J. a leading question: "What do you plan to do with your fourth car?"

In addition to the three cars qualified by himself, George Snider, and Donnie Allison, Foyt had a fourth machine. It was numbered 14. Foyt decided to give it to McElreath. His crew worked until midnight preparing the car.

Not just any driver could have spurred Foyt to such action. First of all, the forty-two-year-old McElreath was a fellow Texan. He had driven once before at the Speedway for Foyt in 1968 when he had placed fourteenth despite a long pit stop. McElreath had been named the Speedway's Rookie of the Year in 1962. In eight starts at the track, he had placed sixth or better four times. In 1966, he lost a minute in the pits when his engine stalled. He finished that race in third, fifty seconds behind the winner. Jimmy McElreath watched from the pits as the car's owner took number 14 out for some shakedown laps. Almost immediately, A. J. had the racer moving 167 miles per hour.

Bentley Warren meanwhile practiced in car number 35; the one Al Loquasto had pushed into the wall the day before. Its nose cone was newly mended and repainted. Three mechanics were bent examining the car's suspension. One of them looked up at Warren. "Is it easy enough to steer?"

The twenty-nine-year-old driver nodded his head. Like many rookies who wanted exposure and experience at the Speedway, he probably would have agreed to drive the car if it meant steering it by ropes in each hand.

Farther down the pit area, Bill Simpson rolled into the pits driving the Weinberger Homes Special 45. He had just gone 163.7 mph. "I thought I was attached to a rocket," he told mechanic Dick Oeffinger. He thus became the car's fourth driver, after Charlie Glotzbach, Al Miller, and Tony Adamowicz (who, after being bumped on Saturday, had driven it several laps). But later Simpson skidded the car into the infield after an oil line burst, covering him with oil. When the safety guards sprayed Simpson with their fire extinguishers, many people thought they were seeing a replay from Tuesday when Simpson had set himself on fire.

At noon Bill Puterbaugh moved onto the track to qualify in number 90, Mike Mosley's backup car. Nearby, Sam Posey sat on the pit wall in stocking feet. As Puterbaugh moved past on his first warm-up lap, Posey walked toward where his mechanics were tinkering with the suspension. Suddenly he turned, realizing he had forgotten his shoes. Puterbaugh didn't reach sufficient speed, so he drove back into the pits without taking the flag. Posey, having retrieved his shoes, breathed on the visor of his helmet. He polished it with a rag. Nobody else stood in line to qualify. "You about ready to go, Sam?" said one of the crewmen. "They're going to open the track for practice."

Posey put on his helmet, then took it off. He walked over to the pit wall for a sip of iced tea. Then he put the helmet back on. "The track is now opened for practice," announced Harlan Fengler over the loudspeaker. Posey climbed into his car.

Denny Zimmerman watched as blocks were installed so he could fit inside the cockpit of the Wynn's Spitfire 98, the car abandoned by

Billy Vukovich. Zimmerman stood three inches shorter than the former driver. Larry Dickson practiced in Gary Bettenhausen's backup car.

Tony Adamowicz sat nearby. John Cannon walked past him and stopped. "Find anything yet?" asked Cannon. Adamowicz shook his head.

At 12:30 p.m. Fengler ordered the track cleared of cars. Jigger Sirois wanted to make a qualifying attempt in the turbine car. Howard Millican walked to the end of the straightaway carrying the rolled-up yellow flag. He still had it rolled after Sirois had taken four sub-160 qualifying laps. Nevertheless, that would be the day's fifth fastest time, earning $300 for the car. Jigger's contract with owner Jack Adams called for him to receive 50 percent of all prize money. Adams told Jigger to keep the entire $300 check. It was the only money that Jigger Sirois received for his month's work at the Speedway.

Following the attempt, a television interviewer asked Jigger why he had accepted the speed even though it obviously would not get him into the race. "Well, the crew has worked very hard with the car all this month," the driver politely explained. "The owner spent a lot of money on it, so I was going to prove what the car would do with its present setup."

"Really though," prodded the interviewer, "what do you feel you have accomplished?"

"Pardon me?" said Jigger, as though he didn't believe the question.

"I say, what really do you feel you have accomplished?"

Jigger glared at the interviewer for a moment, then walked away. The interviewer turned to face his television camera and smiled: "That was Jigger Sirois."

With the qualification attempt over, practice continued. At 1:22 p.m., Gary Bettenhausen's backup car crashed, mangling its radiator and one wheel. The tow truck dumped the wrecked car in front of the Thermo King garage. "What happened?" asked one spectator. "Did Dickson put it into the wall?"

"Dickson wasn't driving," explained a mechanic. "Adamowicz was driving."

Next to the car, Tony Adamowicz, unhurt, looked glum and embarrassed. Sam Posey stood next to him. The two stared at the brown fluid leaking out of the radiator. "I feel terrible," said Tony.

Larry Dickson walked over and patted Adamowicz on the shoulder. Then Dickson crossed to the Weinberger garage to see if maybe they wanted another driver for Charlie Glotzbach's former car.

On the track Jim Hurtubise blew an engine. Wally Dallenbach practiced in his backup car. Kevin Bartlett, Sam Sessions, and Dick Simon had times slower than his, but Dallenbach wanted to be ready in case he got bumped from the field. Sam Sessions waited by the side of the track, watching the cars go around, nervously eyeing a stopwatch in his hand.

Shortly before three, Sam Posey was practicing again. Fire started coming from his engine. Another driver passed and waved at him. Posey, who hadn't realized the danger until that moment, pulled quickly into the infield. The fire was not serious. Bill Simpson climbed into the car driven earlier by Carlos Pairetti.

Finally, A. J. Foyt finished his shakedown laps and, convinced car 14 was ready, handed it to Jimmy McElreath. Earlier in the day a bearing had failed, damaging the engine. "They put in a new engine like it had zippers," commented McElreath. After a half dozen laps, McElreath reached 167 mph. The midday heat made it a poor time for qualifying. Nevertheless, Foyt said, "Let's go."

They pushed the car to the line, and the crowd, which had seen very little action up to this moment, stirred in their seats. A. J. Foyt stalked behind his car, chewing gum as the USAC inspectors made one last examination. He finally bent and gave some last-minute instructions to McElreath, sitting in the cockpit.

The engine started. As McElreath sped off, Foyt grabbed the yellow flag and ran toward the far end of the runway. When Foyt returned, still at a run, he was smiling, and Kevin Bartlett no longer had a place on the starting grid. McElreath's four lap average was 166.821 mph.

Andy Granatelli stood near the entrance to Gasoline Alley as Foyt passed. Foyt, the owner, had qualified four cars into the thirty-three-car field. Andy held up four fingers and shouted: "Hey, A. J. Twenty-nine more to go!" Foyt walked back to his garage, where several of his crew were watching a telecast of the Charlotte 600. The race had gone 275 miles.

"Who's in front?" Foyt asked. When they told him Donnie Allison, A. J. smiled again.

Back on the track, Sammy Sessions, now only the thirty-third fastest qualifier, continued fingering his stopwatch. Steve Krisiloff worked with Rolla Vollstedt, preparing car 21 for John Cannon. Kevin Bartlett waited in 96. Al Miller stood in the infield, just watching. He had his helmet in case anybody suddenly needed him. Bobby Grim occupied the cockpit of car 72. Jigger Sirois had crashed it the day before. But nobody seemed eager to qualify.

Just before five, Sam Posey broke the spell. Three other cars immediately jumped in line behind him. Posey's engine caught, died, then he rushed off grinding his gears. The green flag dropped, and Posey sailed around the first turns and into the back straightaway, seeming to run very fast. He moved very low through Turn Three—too low. His nose hit the grass. The machine skidded up and into the outside wall, bouncing off it twice. Debris covered the turn and, as the yellow light came on, the drivers waiting in line realized that the hour remaining would be cut by the time the cleanup took. It suddenly became very late in May.

When the green light flashed again a half hour later, Kevin Bartlett sat in his cockpit at the front of the line. And he sat there for two minutes as crew chief Jerry Eisert tried to start the engine—without success. They pushed Bartlett out of the way and back to the end of the line. Tom Carnegie announced over the loudspeaker that Donnie Allison's car had won the Charlotte 600, although not with Allison at the wheel. The heat had proved so intense that he had to be relieved less than a hundred miles from the finish by Lee Roy Yarbrough.

Bill Puterbaugh took several warm-up laps but again failed to find any speed. Denny Zimmerman in 99 drove four laps at an average speed of 158.912 mph, third fastest of the day and worth $600. John Cannon went three laps, but Vollstedt raised the yellow flag. Meanwhile back in line, Steve Krisiloff was sitting in the Weinberger car, its fifth driver of the month. Jim Hurtubise's crew had spent the last two-and-a-half hours frantically installing a new engine in his car. They pushed it in line behind Bartlett and Cannon. Hurtubise glanced at his watch: "We've only got eight minutes. Ain't no way possible."

Arnie Knepper raced around the track at that moment, hitting speeds better than 165 mph, and seemed as though he might yet qualify. Sam Sessions watched as Knepper raced past on his fourth qualifying lap and forgot to push the button on his stopwatch. If he had, he would have seen that Knepper failed to make the 500 field by .053 mph.

Larry Dickson rolled out in Carlos Pairetti's car and ran four slow laps. Denny Zimmerman sat on the line in car 50. The people in the stands already had begun moving toward the exits when the starting pistol poked out the window of the control tower. It went off at six, and no excitement remained at Indianapolis except for the race itself.

The pace car; some second guesses

At 8:15 a.m. Monday morning, a single car circled the Indianapolis Speedway. Rodger Ward sat in the driver's seat of the white Oldsmobile 4-4-2 convertible, which on race day would lead the field of thirty-three drivers two laps around the track before the green flag dropped.

Even driving a pace car takes practice. Ward would have to hit 120 miles per hour to stay ahead of the throttled-down racers. As recently as 1948, Mauri Rose won the 500 race with a slower average speed. So, Rodger Ward took three swift laps, then climbed into his own car and drove next door to the Speedway golf course to play in the driver's golf tournament. The winner of the tournament, and a new set of clubs, would be Lloyd Ruby. It was his fourth victory in ten years.

At nine, the tourist minibuses moved onto the track for the first time since April 30. The guides drove slowly through Turn One and showed the tourists four black skid marks wiggling up to the wall. The marks had been left by the tires of Al Loquasto as he spun out of control in front of Lloyd Ruby. The two black smudges he left on the wall, however, had been painted over. "We don't want to be reminded of what happened," one race official had commented, "and neither do the drivers." Inside Turn Three a section of infield grass had been ripped loose, a scar left by Sam Posey.

At the north end of the pits, two men lettered the names and numbers of the drivers on the pit walls. One man in a green shirt sitting on a green pillow painted the name Jack Brabham. The other used chalk to lay out the letters for Gary Bettenhausen.

In Gasoline Alley, the Foyt and Granatelli garages bustled with activity as mechanics continued to prepare their cars. Some of the losers had left. Some were packing their gear, ready to go home or go racing elsewhere. Jim Ward continued to work on car number 28, getting it ready to race at Milwaukee in two weeks. No attempt had been made to qualify the car. "We couldn't get it up to speed," Ward explained. "No sense wasting their time."

Al Loquasto, his arms folded, leaned against an oil can in front of his garage. "If they had given me that 35 car at least two days before qualifying, I would have put it in the show," he said. "That car had a lot left in it. I took it out and in nine laps cranked it up to one hundred sixty-five, but I didn't have the time, and I was in a hurry, and this is one thing you can't do here. You don't rush this place." Loquasto shrugged. "It's the old story: maintaining your cool. On Saturday I didn't maintain my cool."

At the other end of Gasoline Alley, crew chief Dick Oeffinger sat atop his workbench, one arm resting across the handle of a jack, and stared out into space. "We knew when we came here with Charlie Glotzbach," he said, "that we would have to qualify the first weekend or not at all because of his stockcar commitments. Things worked good the first part of the month. He got his driver's test in and got up to almost one hundred sixty-five mph. Then he spun twice and never did seem to reach speed again. Didn't hit anything or hurt the car, but I guess he was a little leery of it after that."

Oeffinger released the handle of the jack and shook his head. "We weren't up to speed the first weekend, so we didn't even try to qualify. Then Mr. Weinberger contacted Al Miller and we ran him all that week. We left the line on Saturday but never did take the green flag. We hired Bill Simpson on Sunday and he did real good. He got up to one hundred sixty-three point eight. First turbo-Offy he ever had driven. Then his oil pressure gauge ruptured. I think if we had a couple of more days to work with him, he would have gotten the job done." Dick Oeffinger shook his head once more.

Howard Millican walked into the garage carrying a damaged part in one hand. He wondered if Dick could lend him a similar part. Dick didn't have that part. "You got enough help on race day?" Dick asked Howard, as he was going out the door.

"Yeah," said Howard, "I'm OK." He paused in the doorway for a moment. "But maybe it's not the right kind. I'll talk to you a little later."

Dick Oeffinger nodded and remained seated on his workbench, staring out the open door.

.

Sam Posey compares tracks

The twenty-sixth of May was Sam Posey's twenty-sixth birthday. He did not celebrate it in Indianapolis, however, but in his home in Sharon, Connecticut.

Immediately after his accident late Sunday afternoon, Posey had ridden sitting up in an ambulance to the field hospital for a mandatory checkup. The doctors pronounced him fit. He returned to trackside to talk with several members of the press, then rushed to the airport to catch a flight to Boston.

Posey expected to test his Dodge Challenger at Bryar, New Hampshire, on Monday, but the car wasn't ready. So, he returned later that day to his home in Sharon to rest.

"I came down that back chute feeling great," said Sam Posey, recalling his Sunday crash. "I thought I was making it into the show. By that time in May, you know what rpms you need to get what kind of lap speed. I was getting more rpms down the back chute because of adjustments we had just made in the blower. The previous two turns I drifted it flat against the wall, taking the throttle early, and it was a terrific experience. When I came into Turn Three, I left the braking to the same point that I had before, or maybe a little deeper. The hassle was the extra speed coupled with some bumps.

"There is a little hump right at the start of the three turn. Then after that, there's almost like a washboard effect. Here's the thing: When I'm driving at the Speedway, I make a tremendous effort to do what Denny Hulme told me. He talked to me before my rookie test and said: 'Look ahead around the corner. The turns are huge, and your eye has to roam ahead or else you don't get the proper trajectory. If you look right in front of you, the way you do in road racing, you'll never get on the turn fast enough. You won't sense it's coming to an end.'

"But looking ahead means that you can't follow the exact contour of the road with your eye. So, the only people who can go really quick at Indy are the guys who have been there often. They know the bumps and ripples in the track without actually having to look. They just feel it. It's the way I know some of the road racing tracks, such as Lime Rock or Bryar. My mind is clear for other things. As a result, I go quick.

"At Indy I promised myself that I would not drive over my head. It was a matter of experience. A rookie can get away with fast speeds for a lap or two, maybe a few turns at a time, *if* he just keeps gathering it up all the time. I don't think you can keep it up for long until you get a feeling for where the ripples are. But there was the excitement of the moment, so I forgot that rule—unfortunately.

"Or fortunately. The car wouldn't have gotten in the show. It wasn't fast enough. It took a psychological peak for me to get it going fast, but at the same time that peak brought on the accident."

Sam Posey paused as though trying to replay the accident once more in his mind. "I was out of control the minute I left the straightaway. By the time I reached the grass, I was going sideways, then I remember the nose cone going over my left shoulder.

"I clouted the wall a pretty good one. I guess the car skidded again, then it rolled back into the middle of the track. I jumped out of the car in case it caught fire, but the track was banked so I lost my balance. And those crash crews are so fantastic that someone almost caught me.

"I had time to walk around the car once and look at it. Then Harlan Fengler appeared in the pace car, and he put it right to me: 'What happened?' For a moment I considered all possible manner of wild excuses, then I just told him outright that I had made a mistake. He nodded, asked if I was all right, and drove off."

Sam Posey rose from his chair and walked to the window. He looked out at the Connecticut countryside. Eight miles down the road was the Lime Rock racetrack, where he had experienced considerably more success than he had in Indianapolis during the month of May. "A lot of people may think driving at Indianapolis is easy," Sam continued, "because there are four nearly identical turns, but that's not true. In road racing we are used to operating at maybe ninety-five percent efficiency. With the great variety of turns, there is no hope to get a car set up to do every turn right. There will be a lot of compromises.

"But at Indy, you set up the car to do one thing: turn left. Thus, it can be more sensitive. You're talking about maybe ninety-nine percent efficiency. Its limit is higher in that one turn than we are used to coping with in any one turn of a road course. The higher the limit, the tougher a car is to drive. Obviously if the limit of the car is very low, like in Go-Kart racing at five miles per hour, the number of people who can drive it to that limit increases enormously … But at Indy, when it comes to driving full tilt into one of those turns, you are only talking, at the moment, of about three or four people in the entire world who can do it. A second echelon of maybe a dozen more are pretty good.

"I was never particularly tense during the month. Tension is the big enemy of a lot of people at the Speedway. It detracts from their performance. On the other hand, I'm very anxious to achieve success. I don't take Indy so casually that I'm not concerned about the way I left—on a note of failure.

"One's whole career at Indy can be determined by what you do the first couple of years. Peter Revson did well there his first year, so everybody will say he's terrific for a long time. If you do something stupid early, it takes a long time to live it down. Well, I've done something stupid, but people knew I was going very fast. The door is still open for me. So, I'm going to try my best to see that if I come back next year it will be with a good machine."

Practice for the lucky thirty-three

For three hours beginning Wednesday morning, the thirty-three qualifiers for the Indianapolis 500-mile race returned to the track for one last practice session. Al Unser had the fastest time, with 169.7 miles per hour. Johnny Rutherford's car briefly caught fire because of an overheated turbocharger. Art Pollard punctured a tire when he ran over a drill bit. Dick Simon kept his practice speeds under 160 mph. "We're afraid we might break something," he admitted. "We don't have any spare parts."

For two hours in the afternoon, the crew practiced pit stops, fueling the cars, and changing tires. When Al Unser's Johnny Lightning crew practiced ten minutes past the three o'clock deadline, USAC assessed the team a penalty fine.

Parnelli Jones had to pay $25. Four days later he would reflect that those ten minutes had been well worth the money.

500 Festival Parade; Mark Donohue

On Thursday evening, 350,000 people crowded the downtown streets of Indianapolis to watch the 500 Festival Parade. The parade featured bands, floats, celebrities, and three astronauts. The stars of the parade, however, were the thirty-three drivers, among them Mark Donohue.

Of all the drivers at the Speedway in May, Donohue probably came closest to matching an astronaut in appearance and temperament. Auto racing is a violent sport. To succeed in it, a driver must know how and when to charge. Many drivers are chargers off the track as well as on.

Mark Donohue, however, is a chunky 180-pounder, who wears his hair crew-cut short and speaks softly. As the month of May progressed, he seemed a man outside the regular circle of Indy veterans.

"I can remember coming to Indianapolis years ago," Donohue recalled, "and never having any great yearning to come back and race. I pretty much made up my mind that this was an area in which I wasn't qualified to be involved."

Born in Summit, New Jersey, Donohue attended school in nearby Elizabeth. Like most young boys, he played neighborhood sports, but he claimed to exhibit little talent. "In games I was always one of the last ones to get chosen," he recalls. At Brown University he took part in dramatics and served as manager of the soccer team. He also majored in mechanical engineering and drove his own Corvette in hill climbs. He won the first race he entered.

After graduation in 1959, Donohue began driving in amateur sports-car races and won several national championships. The Sports Car Club of America named him its Driver of the Year in 1965. By this time, he had attracted the attention of Roger Penske.

Penske, only a few years older than Donohue, also had raced sports cars. He won with such ease that he soon saw little challenge left in remaining a driver. He entered business, first as a Chevrolet dealer in the Philadelphia area and then as a renter of Hertz cars in five cities. When he decided to organize a racing team, he hired Mark Donohue as his driver.

In 1966, Donohue placed second in the Can-Am challenge series. He won six out of eight races in the United States Road Racing Championship series in 1967 and placed third in Can-Am. The next two years Donohue drove a Camaro in the Trans-Am series, winning the manufacturer's championships for Chevrolet.

He also returned to the Speedway—this time as a driver, not a spectator. Donohue qualified for the 500 in fourth place in 1969 and by lap 172 was running third, when his magneto failed. An eleven-minute pit stop corrected the problem and he eventually finished seventh. Sportswriters named him the Speedway's Rookie of the Year.

On Sunday the seventeenth, after he had qualified, Mark Donohue had run several morning practice laps to see how his car responded with a full fuel load. That afternoon Penske's team removed the engine and placed it on a plane for Los Angeles to be overhauled by Falconer and Dunn, who also prepared Andretti's engines. The engine was returned by the end of the week, and Donohue practiced again with it in the car during the second weekend of qualifications. "We didn't want to leave everything until the last minute," Penske explained.

On Monday and Tuesday, Donohue worked, testing his Javelin at Bryar for a race to be run the day after the 500. In the meantime, Penske's crew took the Indianapolis racer to a Sunoco depot in nearby Clermont, Indiana. They spent five hours doing wet runs with their refueling equipment. "A fast pit stop is worth free time on the straightaway," says Penske.

Donohue returned from Bryar to Indianapolis on Wednesday for a final day of practice. He needed the practice to reaccustom himself to the car. He found it easy to go from the Indy car to the Javelin but hard to return. "The Javelin is a slower car and not as precise. There's more wheel movement, more pedal travel, and larger slip angles. It's difficult to come back."

On Thursday he stopped at the garage to check the suspension and assure himself that the alignment was correct. Then he returned to his motel room to change for that evening's parade.

"From a physical standpoint, racing doesn't demand a great deal of strength. It's more concentration and finesse than anything else. Mark has both," Penske says.

Mark Donohue also possessed one other attribute important at Indianapolis: staying power. In the past two years he had finished better than 50 percent of the races he started. In the 500, victory most often goes not to the fastest drivers but to the drivers who drive close enough to the lead to be ready when the equipment of the fast drivers breaks down. If anything seemed certain, it was that Mark Donohue would become the winner of the Indianapolis 500. The only question remaining was: Would it be this year?

Drivers' meeting with Fengler; some instructions

A steady drizzle fell on Friday afternoon. A drivers' meeting had been scheduled for the grandstand at one o'clock, but nobody wanted to sit out in the rain. The drivers stood in the doors of their garages and hoped it wouldn't rain tomorrow.

At 1:30 p.m. the meeting was rescheduled to the grandstand across the track. The thirty-three drivers settled into a neat line, three abreast, in the same order in which they would start the race. Their crew members and several celebrities sat nearby. The remainder of the crowd consisted of friends, relatives, and racing fans.

Mario Andretti received a plaque for his victory a year before. Al Unser accepted a trophy for winning the pole. Arnie Knepper got $500 for being the thirty-fourth driver. A number of gifts (including a gold-plated tool set) went to Tony Hulman, honoring his twenty-fifth anniversary as Speedway owner.

The rain continued to fall. Minibuses jammed with tourists moved down the straightaway. Across the track a truck pulled into the pit of A. J. Foyt and unloaded a fuel tank. The name FOYT had been painted in bright white letters on the runway. No other driver had his pit so embellished, but tomorrow morning the name would be painted over.

Harlan Fengler gave the drivers the instructions they had heard many times before. Only seven crew members would be allowed on the apron; only six could work on the car. The race would start at twelve noon. There would be a parade lap, then a pace lap at 120 to 125 miles per hour. Fengler wanted a one-hundred-foot cushion between rows.

"Let me warn you, Johnny and A. J.," said the chief steward, "don't jump out before the start."

One hundred and one laps constitutes an official race. If rain stops the race before lap 101, they would restart; otherwise, the finish was official. Everybody would have to make three stops for fuel. "Stay above the white lines unless you need to go down there," advised Fengler. "That's no place to be running." If the race is stopped before two laps, they would reform; if more than two laps, the race would begin again in single file.

When the meeting ended, the drivers returned to their garages or motel rooms to await the next day. Mark Donohue was one of them. After dinner he turned on Channel Eight to watch an hour-long special on tomorrow's race. Announcer Jim Wilson was asking A. J. Foyt how he drove the 500 race.

"Last year I tried to pace myself," A. J. said, "and mechanical failure still frowned on us. So, I think if it's your day, you can run flat out and live. That's the way to win."

Foyt talked about passing the other drivers. He said he could run within five or six inches of Andretti or the Unsers. He knew what to expect of them. Wilson asked about oil on the track.

"I've had it very slick," A. J. replied. "Sometimes it is. Sometimes it isn't. It depends on how much oil is leaking. It can be you as well as anybody else. But a good handling chassis is the key to being successful here.

"I'm raising the gear, which will probably hurt me at the start of the race," said Foyt. "And I'm setting up for an oily track. I just feel that with the weather being hot, there are going to be a lot of liquids on the racetrack. In case the track gets slick, I don't want to push the front end. So, at the start of the race, I might be a little loose, but as the track gets slicker I think I'll be in better shape."

When A. J. Foyt answered that last question, Mark Donohue, Brown University, class of 1959, watching the interview on the television set in his motel room, decided that he had just received a lesson in auto mechanics from a high school dropout.

The Indy 500 Race

Only a half hour before the scheduled noon start of the Indianapolis 500, thirty-three cars sat parked on the main straightaway, many of them under plastic covers. It was the thirtieth day of May, and it was raining.

Throughout the grandstands and infield of the Indianapolis Motor Speedway, 300,000 people waited, hoping the rain would stop. Many in the infield had waited all night to be first in line. When the gates opened at 6:00 a.m., the Speedway suffered its first accident. Three motorcycle riders collided rushing through the tunnel under the track. They were taken to the hospital.

The rain did stop, and Johnny Rutherford moved toward his car. He bent to look beneath the radiator and rose with a smudge on one knee. The track was wet—too wet for the race to begin at noon. This meant waiting and more tension for the drivers. ABC television announcer Chris Economaki asked Johnny how he planned to handle the first turn.

"If the lead comes easy, I'll take it," Johnny replied. "If it becomes a hassle and if I have to hang it out to get in there first, I won't risk it."

Al Unser stood near the track wall talking to his brother Bobby and mechanic George Bignotti. Al had gone to bed around ten and had slept soundly. "I don't care if I get into the first turn ahead of everyone else," he told a reporter from the *Indianapolis Star*. "I wouldn't mind letting someone else set the pace for a while."

Al walked over to his car and reached beneath the plastic sheet for his helmet. He began polishing his visor with a rag. Most drivers wear a plastic cover over their regular visors for the first few laps as protection against the sand and dirt kicked up at the start. After a few laps the track becomes cleaner and they discard the pitted covers.

A Firestone engineer passed and wished Al Unser luck. "Thank you," he replied automatically.

A. J. Foyt climbed into the cockpit of his machine, tested the pedals, and climbed out again. A safety patrolman handed him a program. A. J. smiled and signed it.

Just before noon, Harlan Fengler inspected the track and described Turn Two as too wet. He expected a half hour delay. He would look again in fifteen minutes, and in the meantime the drivers could run their engines for five minutes to warm the oil. The rumble of engines soon filled the air.

Dick Simon, interviewed over the public address system, commented: "I can honestly say this is the proudest moment of my life." He returned to his car in the last row, slapped his hands together, and sat down on a tire. "I've got more butterflies than I've ever had right now," said the former ski jumper and sky diver.

At 12:25 p.m. Harlan Fengler announced that the race could begin, so the drivers began to climb into their race cars. Over the public address system Saverio Saridis sang "Back Home Again in Indiana." Few of the drivers heard him. At the head of the straightaway, Tony Hulman stood in the rear seat of the pace car, microphone held to his mouth, surrounded by photographers, and gestured dramatically as he said the words: "Gentlemen, start your engines." The crowd cheered.

Even as Hulman spoke, George Snider's engine began to wind. *BRRR-RUMMP!* It caught. One by one the other engines started. *RUMP! ROOMP! ROOOMP!* As they did, the crewmen standing beside the cars raised their arms to signal their readiness. The engine noises rippled against the grandstands. Then the pace car began to move. The ripples suddenly merged to one harsh roar as the cars lurched forward down the track.

Electricity seemed to fill the air. The moment was near when all the energy stored at the Speedway during thirty days of preparation would be released. The start of the Indianapolis 500 is probably the most exciting moment in sports. It may also be the most dangerous. Within a matter of seconds, thirty-three cars, racing three abreast at speeds over 150 miles per hour, must shuffle and align themselves into single file. The groove is only one car wide. Following the mass first lap crash in 1966, Speedway officials increased the distance between rows to one hundred feet. That helped reduce the risk at the start. It did not eliminate it.

"Here they are!" shouted announcer Tom Carnegie, as the pace car followed by eleven rows of brightly colored racing automobiles moved past on the parade lap. People in the crowd waved. Several cars see-sawed back and forth trying to get in position. And on Turn Two, it began to rain again.

"It was raining pretty good," Johnny Rutherford recalled later. "We were getting water on our face shields and helmets. A. J., Al, and I were looking at each other, wondering what to do. We tried to get the pace car's attention by holding our palms up to signal rain."

But Rodger Ward already was in touch with Fengler. On the back stretch, the observer reported that the rain had stopped and the track was dry. Fengler told Ward: "We'll start the race." Ward began to pick up speed. As he rounded Turn Four he headed full speed into the pits, then glanced to his right, surprised.

Starter Pat Vidan had not waved the green flag.

Johnny Rutherford figured it was because of the rain. Mario Andretti at first thought some of the rear cars had moved out of line. Then he looked to the outside and for the first time realized that Jim Malloy was no longer next to him. The lead cars circled the track and finally came past Malloy's dented car surrounded by firemen and safety guards. Mario worried whether he had crowded Malloy into the wall coming out of Turn Four.

Malloy had gone into the wall, but not because of Mario Andretti. The chain of events that caused the accident started earlier in the week.

During Wednesday's carburation tests, Malloy had planned to practice with a full fuel load. He had not done so earlier because his engine was being overhauled. But clutch problems developed on Wednesday. He only went six practice laps, none of them with a fueled car.

The Offenhauser engine then developed valve problems. On Friday night before the race, mechanic Paul Brooks and his crew had worked late replacing the valves. No time remained for further tests. They had no way to anticipate how their car might handle under full power and with the weight of seventy gallons of fuel pushing the right rear wheel on a turn to the left.

As Malloy rounded Turn Four on the pace lap, his outside position caused him to lag behind the two drivers inside him in row three. The field still was moving slowly. As he turned into the straightaway, Malloy stepped on the throttle to pull even for the start. At that instant a valve malfunctioned. The sudden surge of power placed all the thrust on the right rear wheel. The radius rod snapped loose from the tub.

Mike Mosely, outside on the fourth row, was following Malloy when it happened. "The car just jumped sideways on him," said Mosely later. He swerved quickly to the left and cut under Malloy. Back in row nine, Jack Brabham saw what happened and decided Malloy could never save the car. Like most other drivers back in the pack, he hit his brakes.

When the radius rod snapped, the right rear wheel moved out of line. The back end slid right. Malloy countered by turning the front end right. "I had to put the car up against the wall to keep it from spinning in front of everybody," he recalled. "I got my speed down, but when I pulled off the wall the car looped anyway." By that time the rear drivers had slowed enough to avoid hitting Malloy as he spun into the infield grass.

Malloy's car was brought into the pits, dangling limply from the rear of a tow truck labeled EDDIE'S 24-HOUR SERVICE. Despite the collision, the damage didn't seem too great. But repairing the car in time for the restart was impossible. "I was disappointed," said Malloy, "but if it had popped loose in the number one turn when we had gotten up real speed, it really could have been disastrous." He later received a check for $13,677.48, thirty-third place in a race he had not even started.

* * *

Thirty-two cars resumed their positions on the starting grid. Harlan Fengler allowed the crews to refill their tanks. As Johnny Rutherford waited beside his car for restart, he felt a new confidence. He realized he could easily grab the lead.

During the false start, he had surged ahead of both the other two front row drivers. "The turbo came on right up to snuff," he recalled, "and I pulled both of them down the straightaway." Foyt, who had raised his gear ratio for all-day running, couldn't match Rutherford's pickup. Al Unser stayed close, but Rutherford figured his higher position would give him the angle going into the first corner. Unless Unser could get at least a half car length ahead and force him to back off, Rutherford expected to come out on top across the short chute.

Tony Hulman stood again in the pace car, only this time it was: "Gentlemen, *restart* your engines." Once more there was a parade lap and a pace lap. Coming down the main straightaway, the lead drivers had one foot on the throttle and the other on the brakes. Johnny Rutherford raced his engine to 5,000 rpm. The chassis of his yellow Patrick Petroleum Special vibrated as the engine fought to overcome the drag of the brakes.

The green flag waved.

Rutherford removed his foot from the brakes and stomped harder on the throttle. His racer leaped forward. As he reached the end of the straightaway, his rear wheel was even with the front wheel of Al Unser inside him. And he had the high line.

Unser backed off and Rutherford led through Turn One.

A. J. Foyt trailed nearly three car lengths behind the two leaders. Mark Donohue, who had shot forward from the center of the second row, moved behind him to the inside. Art Pollard cut cleanly down in front of a lagging Roger McCluskey to a position two car lengths behind Donohue. Mario Andretti positioned himself outside Pollard's right rear wheel. Bobby Unser and the rest of the field trailed.

Mike Mosely took off at the start of the race in fourth gear. When he reached the end of the straightaway, he found that he had pulled ahead of Dan Gurney and George Snider on his inside. "I just moved over as slowly as I could to get down in the groove," he said.

Back on the inside of row nine, Lloyd Ruby had begun with no particular strategy. "Starting that far back you can't have any," he said later. "The only thing you can do is run flat out. At the start of the race, I was pinned down, so when I got to the first turn, I moved out and passed two or three cars on the outside. Then in the number two turn

I passed a couple more. I couldn't tell you who they were. Things were happening too fast."

In his charge to the front from the twenty-fifth position, Ruby held a double edge. The ten-race veteran drove a machine clearly better than most of the dozen cars immediately ahead of him. And five of those dozen drivers had run only one 500 race or none. Only five-race veteran Joe Leonard in the sixth row seemed anywhere near a match for Lloyd Ruby. "A lot of fellows think the inside is the only place you can run," says Ruby, "but actually on the first lap you're not running that fast. You're only up to about one hundred forty by the first turn. At that speed you can move out of the groove."

George Follmer remembered Ruby zooming past him on the short chute between Turns Three and Four. When asked if it were possible to pass cars at that point on the track, Follmer replied, "Lloyd Ruby can." By the end of lap one, Ruby had moved up ten positions.

And Al Unser had moved ahead one position. At the first turn Unser could see Rutherford high and ahead of him. "I didn't want to see him hung up like that," Al recalled. "It might have started a crash. So, I backed off, got on the brakes, and let him go."

Unser let Rutherford go only so far. He moved in on his tail coming through the first two turns. As the two cars came out into the back straightaway, Unser moved down to the inside and blew right past Rutherford and into the lead. Al's burst of speed convinced Johnny that passing him again might be impossible. He decided to concentrate on staying near him, hoping to regain the lead at the first pit stop.

Dick Simon in the back row dropped back quickly at the start. He wanted to finish in the top ten, but he had never run more than six laps in succession on the Speedway track. "It was my first time," he said, "and I guess I had an early fear of somebody getting in trouble in front of me. Since I was in the last row, I was able to backtrack a little without bothering anybody. I watched the temperatures and they stayed the same. I gained a little more confidence each lap, so I began pushing the car harder."

Donnie Allison also started the same way. "I ran slow at first to get the feel of the race," he said. "Then I stepped up my pace. The one thing I didn't want to do was get involved in an accident."

But Lloyd Ruby charged. By lap five he had moved to tenth. Now, a large gap separated him from the front runners. Moving relentlessly, he soon found himself running alone.

On the eighth lap Carl Williams suddenly felt the fourth gear pop loose in his McLaren car. "And then the freight train went by," he said. He had to drive the rest of the race in third gear.

Mel Kenyon's car also developed problems. After a few laps the steering wheel of the Sprite Special began vibrating. It was a steady vibration that continued on the straightaway and the turns. Later Kenyon would theorize that one of the balance weights on his right rear wheel had come off.

Kenyon, of course, steered with his crippled left hand by means of a socket glove that fit over a knob on the steering wheel. The hand had poor circulation. Soon the steady vibration caused it to fall asleep.

On lap twelve a piston failed in Greg Weld's engine, and he dropped out of the race. He placed thirty-second, ahead of Malloy. On that lap, Bobby Unser cut ahead of Mario Andretti. On lap eighteen, George Follmer pulled into the pits and climbed out of his car. The water hose had rubbed against the pulley. It soon cut a hole in it. Follmer placed thirty-first. But now his STP teammate also had problems.

Only a few laps earlier Andretti moved past Donohue and then Foyt. He held fifth place. "The car felt comfortable," recalled Mario, "then all of a sudden it just changed." The rear end began swinging loose on the turns and Andretti found himself fighting to keep up with the front pack. He saw Roger McCluskey come by him and then Lloyd Ruby.

Ruby came high past McCluskey and Foyt on the main straightaway, but he was too high to get back down into the groove. He had to brake to keep from going into the wall. Car owner Gene White watched with horror. "When he went into number one, I just automatically looked around for the yellow caution light to go on. He got so high in the gray stuff; the sweepers don't even go there."

Ruby finally got past the two other drivers. Now clear of the slow runners, he had learned he no longer could pass at will.

Art Pollard had moved into third shortly after the start of the race. Although having quickly lost contact with Unser and Rutherford, he nevertheless led the second pack. Then just as he passed the starting line going into the twenty-ninth lap, a cloud of smoke burst from his engine. A piston had failed, the same trouble that had halted his team-mate Greg Weld. "We used untried pistons, and they just didn't hold up," explained crew chief Grant King later. "The patterns we had for our normal piston were lost, so we had to take a gamble. It just didn't pay off." Pollard placed thirtieth.

A piece from Pollard's exhaust pipe cracked loose, dropping onto the track. The yellow flag came out.

The race cars slowed under the caution light, and several drivers faced with problems decided to pit. One was Gary Bettenhausen, but he ran right past his pit and had to come around another time. Then he waited nineteen minutes for a wheel spindle to be changed.

Mario Andretti also pitted early. After his car began handling badly, he noticed that one of the three Dzus fittings holding his hood in place had loosened. "I figured the trouble was aerodynamics," he said. "Maybe air was rushing under the hood and upsetting the handling of the car." The STP crew quickly fastened the button and covered it with tape. They also refueled the car. Andretti moved confidently back out onto the track.

In an earlier interview with Peter Manso in *Car & Driver*, Andretti had discussed how he left the pits: "You've got to get yourself in the right frame of mind. Never, never go out with a blank mind like you're all by yourself. You've always got to be aware of what's going on around you, other traffic and so on. As you pull out of the pits and build up speed, nothing quite scares you more than a guy going by at two hundred miles an hour. You're only doing maybe a hundred, in second gear. You're in second and get third in between the short chute and the second turn and go one third of the way down the back stretch before putting it into fourth."

Andretti did all those things—and almost lost his car on the second turn. The loose Dzus button had not been the cause of his problems.

At that point, Gordon Johncock dropped out of the race. "The engine just gave up," he explained. (A piston had broken.) Johncock placed twenty-eighth, right ahead of Bruce Walkup who had had engine trouble a lap earlier.

* * *

Dan Gurney also was plagued by vibrations. He pulled in for his first stop on lap forty-five, certain that something was about to fall off his car. His crew told him they could find nothing wrong. He pulled back onto the track, but his long pit stop caused him to slip from ninth place at lap forty to twelfth on lap sixty.

By the forty-ninth lap, Johnny Rutherford still had Al Unser in sight. "He got less than a short chute ahead of me," Johnny recalled. Rutherford planned to wait until Unser pitted for fuel, then run one or two laps before pitting himself. With a light fuel load, he could run very fast. When Unser came out of his pits with a full fuel load, it would take him one or two laps to regain speed. A quick pit stop might permit Rutherford to regain the lead or at least move in close enough to pressure the lead driver.

The plan only had one flaw: Johnny Rutherford started to run out of fuel. The engine of his Patrick Petroleum Special began to stutter on the banked Turn Two. It caught again down the back straightaway. On Turns Three and Four the engine stuttered again. Rutherford kicked the car out of gear. As soon as he did, the engine died. He still had enough speed, however, to coast into his pit.

Al Unser also had decided to pit, but suddenly he found Carl Williams coasting slowly down the runway ahead of him with a killed engine. Unser darted to the left and inside of Williams. Further down the pit area a fireman stood, extinguisher poised, outside the rear wheel of another car. For an instant, the front wheel of the Johnny Lightning car aimed directly at the unsuspecting fireman. At the last moment Unser swerved back into the center of the runway. He took fuel and zoomed back onto the track in 18.6 seconds.

Johnny Rutherford still sat waiting. The engine had been restarted. His crew pulled the fuel hoses from the car. They began to push him back toward the track. But the clutch, possibly strained by the stuttering engine as it ran out of fuel, failed to disengage. "I crammed the car in gear," said Johnny. "It coughed, lurched, and it was too much for the engine. It stalled." So did Johnny's hopes for victory. By the time the engine was restarted, he had spent fifty-six seconds in the pit. Instead of leading Unser, Rutherford now found himself a lap behind.

When Unser and Rutherford pitted, A. J. Foyt held the lead, but only for a single lap around the track. On the fiftieth lap he refueled and changed two right tires. It was a clean pit stop, 26.3 seconds according to timers in the press box. They time drivers from the moment they stop to the moment they start.

Apparently Foyt had lost nearly eight seconds on Unser, the leader. But the official timers measure from entrance to exit of the pits. This included the time Unser lost dodging Carl Williams. They timed Unser in forty-three seconds and Foyt in forty-four. Foyt had lost only one second.

With Foyt in the pits, Lloyd Ruby led for two laps. It was the climax of his charge from the twenty-fifth starting position. But smoke had begun to trail from his engine. Pat Vidan showed Ruby the black flag and he came in on the fifty-second lap, giving the lead to Mark Donohue.

Donohue pitted on lap fifty-three. His thirty-nine-second stop, as measured by USAC, bettered that of any other driver and allowed him to gain four seconds on Al Unser. Jack Brabham inherited the lead for one lap (thus earning a $150 lap prize) by virtue of being the last driver to refuel. When Brabham finally pitted, Unser regained the lead on lap fifty-four.

Neither Ruby's crew nor the USAC inspector could find the cause of the smoke. They waved him refueled back onto the track. But the smoke grew denser. Two laps later Pat Vidan black flagged Ruby again. A bearing in the pinion gear had failed, causing oil leakage, the smoke, and eventually a fire as Ruby coasted to a halt in the infield on the backstretch. Ruby climbed out of his burning car and walked quickly away, as though he didn't want to look at it. He had placed only twenty-seventh. "We'll be back," he said later. "I can beat this track yet."

* * *

At that moment, Mel Kenyon sat in the pits having his left arm massaged. The numbness caused by steering wheel vibration had progressed all the way from his hand to above the elbow. "My arm felt just like a piece of wood," admitted Kenyon.

The crew failed to find the cause of the vibration. And as they fueled the car, one of the hoses collapsed. Fuel wouldn't flow through it into the right tank. After nearly a two-minute stop, Kenyon returned to the track with his left tank full and the right tank empty. Now he not only had to contend with the vibration, but the unbalanced load upset the car's handling even more.

By the sixtieth lap, Al Unser held a comfortable seven-second lead over a charging Joe Leonard, who had just moved into second place. Leonard had spent two seconds less time in the pits than his Johnny Lightning teammate. Foyt held third right on Leonard's tail. A five-second gap separated them and the dueling Roger McCluskey and Mark Donohue. Another half lap behind, Mario Andretti battled his car rather than the other drivers. Mike Mosely and Peter Revson followed him closely. Brabham and Rutherford rounded out the top ten.

Two laps later, the day apparently ended for Roger McCluskey. A suspension arm broke. "I felt it go in the one corner," he explained. "I thought at first it was a flat tire, but then across the chute the car started dog tracking. I knew then something more serious was wrong."

McCluskey pulled into the pits and climbed out of his car. He stood glaring at it for a while. Roger finally headed back for the garage to change out of his driving uniform. He placed twenty-fifth.

* * *

Gary Bettenhausen had returned to the track following the long, nineteen-minute pit stop. Two dozen laps later a dropped valve stopped him completely. He placed twenty-sixth.

On the backstretch of the seventy-third lap, Joe Leonard's car began to slow down. Leonard coasted around Turn Four, then stopped just short of the pit entrance. He pushed his car back to the pits, but the crew failed to start it again. George Bignotti diagnosed the problem as magneto failure. "We had a half dozen magnetos back in the garage," Bignotti explained. "We just happened to pick the wrong one to install in Joe's car."

Later, however, the Johnny Lightning crew realized the magneto was not to blame. During the race, Leonard's hand apparently had brushed across the ignition switch, turning it off. The engine, of course, died. By the time anyone discovered the true cause of the problem, the race had ended. Leonard had the dubious honor (considering his twenty-fourth placing) of having driven a single lap faster than any other driver that day. He recorded 167.785 mph on lap fifty. His charge had been almost as spectacular as that of Lloyd Ruby. He had gone from eighteenth at the start to second at one point. He was running a close third when his engine stopped.

* * *

Three minutes after Gary Bettenhausen's engine failed, the longest month in Bill Vukovich's life also ended. A gear failed, the same problem that also had halted Lloyd Ruby. He placed twenty-third.

Peter Revson left the race on lap eighty-seven, when the distributor shaft of his car's magneto broke. He placed twenty-second.

* * *

Meanwhile, Revson's McLaren teammate Carl Williams rolled along in third gear ahead of only three cars on the track: Sam Sessions, Mel Kenyon, and Lee Roy Yarbrough.

The vibration continued to numb Mel Kenyon's hand. Soon it began to throb with pain. But with the fuel level dropping, steering became easier. As Al Unser began lap eighty-nine, Mel came in for his second fuel stop, two laps behind the leader. His crew had repaired the faulty hose. He took a full load of fuel. But just as he headed back to the track, Dick Simon came rushing down the runway.

After his slow start, Simon began to gain confidence in his ability to maneuver in heavy Speedway traffic. He gradually increased his speed. On lap seventy-four he hit 164.926 mph, almost as fast as he had gone while qualifying. As other drivers dropped out of the race, he improved his place, until by lap eighty he was running eleventh.

Simon's pit was at the far end of the runway just ahead of Mel Kenyon's. And he was traveling fast. "I came into the pits rather hot," Simon admitted later. He saw the other driver and planned to pull in front of him. But as he came closer, he realized Kenyon was moving. Simon had to stop quickly enough to duck behind Kenyon or go around one more lap. His engine had coughed several times on the turns from lack of fuel, so he had only one choice. He braked. He spun. He narrowly missed the other driver, who continued onto the track. Simon's crew rushed out and pushed him safely back into the pits for refueling.

Mario Andretti had pitted on the seventy-ninth lap, still plagued by handling problems. His crew removed his right rear tire and put on a new one. Mario went back out and the car handled worse than before. He returned to the pits, and they took off the new tire and put the old one back on again. Dan Gurney, who was following Mario at one point in the race, noticed that his right rear tire was laying down a thin black line of rubber around the turns. By midway through the race, Mario Andretti already had made four pit stops and was running in sixteenth place, barely keeping his car on the track in the turns. "I was an accident waiting to happen," he later said.

Al Unser continued to lead as the race neared the halfway point. But A. J. Foyt followed a mere five seconds behind, content with his strategy to charge late. On the ninety-ninth lap, Foyt's crew signaled for him to pit for fuel. Al Unser prepared to do the same. Any lead change would depend on the relative skills of the two pit crews.

But events moved to conspire against A. J. Foyt. Several laps earlier, Mike Mosely's crew had noticed what looked like a pinhole in his radiator. They decided to wait until the next fuel stop before repairing it. But enough water leaked from Mosely's radiator to cause his engine to overheat badly. He now sat in the pits, out of the race with twenty-first place.

* * *

And at that moment, the engine of George Snider, Foyt's teammate, began to pop and sputter. He pulled into the pits several laps ahead of schedule. Mosely's pit was immediately ahead of Foyt's; Snider's was right behind it.

Unser rushed from the track, followed by Foyt. Foyt stopped, still half on the runway, and glared through his visor at the narrow space available. He could have squeezed in between Mosely and Snider, but nobody in his crew directed him. Only one man gives the signals for the Foyt team, and that man was sitting in the cockpit. Foyt reacted instantly and decided to go around one more time.

George Bignotti stood further down the runway, helping fuel Al Unser's car. When he saw Foyt rush past, he thought in a moment of panic that they had lost the lead. "That's impossible," he said. As Unser returned to the track, the mechanic realized what had happened: Foyt had missed his pit.

On the next lap Foyt's crew guided their boss in smoothly. They connected the fuel hoses. One crewman thrust a jack under the right rear axle and lifted it to examine the tire. With the fuel nozzles removed, Foyt instantly rushed forward again, but his right rear remained up on the jack. The car jerked ahead, its right tire spinning, then *smack!* The jack snapped against the pavement and went spinning into the air. Foyt's car leaped ahead as the jack clattered harmlessly to the cement.

On the next lap, Foyt's crew flashed him the sign: TIRE OK. But Foyt wasn't OK. His pit mistake had padded Al Unser's lead by a full half minute.

By virtue of coasting through the pits, Foyt actually led the 101st lap. That earned him $150. When Foyt finally stopped, Mark Donohue moved in front. But Al Unser, returning to the track, trailed the unpitted Donohue by only a car length. Donohue stayed ahead of Unser long enough to lead for four laps, then finally turned in for fuel. When he returned, the first four drivers were separated by nearly half-lap gaps: Al Unser, Foyt, Donohue, and Gurney.

Mel Kenyon's problems continued to multiply. As his left arm grew more numb, he found himself driving more and more with his right hand. This placed extra pressure on his flexible seat. It began to slide back. And as it slid back, it increased his steering problems! The pain in his injured hand increased to the point where Mel began to worry that the circulation loss might cause him permanent damage. "I didn't think finishing the race was worth the risk, so I pulled in," he said.

Mel's brother Don told him to continue driving until they could locate another driver. They first recruited Gary Bettenhausen. Then Don suddenly recalled that Roger McCluskey also had dropped out of the race. Kenyon was driving the same car that McCluskey had driven during the 1968 season. Car owner Lindsay Hopkins found McCluskey sitting in his garage in Gasoline Alley dressed in sports clothes. "Grab your helmet," Hopkins told him. McCluskey climbed back into his driver's uniform and ran back to the track.

George Snider lasted only a few laps past Foyt's problem pit stop. He placed twentieth. Lee Roy Yarbrough soon quit, taking nineteenth. A cracked header dropped Johnny Rutherford from the race on lap 135. Wally Dallenbach placed seventeenth after going 143 laps.

* * *

By then, only two cars were traveling on the same lap: Unser and Foyt. Behind the wall of the Johnny Lightning pit, George Bignotti stood beside Parnelli Jones. Parnelli held a stopwatch in his hand. "How fast is he going?" Bignotti asked him.

Parnelli told him Al's speed had been 163.7 mph. Parnelli started his watch as Unser passed, then stopped it as Foyt went by. "Thirty-three seconds," Parnelli told Bignotti.

Bignotti signaled the crewman standing by the track who held up a sign to Al: 33. On the next lap, he showed Al a 34, then another 33.

The two leaders headed into the pits on the 151st lap.

Unser looked back calmly over his left shoulder as his crew swarmed around him. The tires showed little wear. The fuel hoses were yanked quickly from the cocks. Al Unser moved out again. As Foyt followed down the runway, Parnelli defiantly waved him past. When Parnelli checked his watch on the next lap, his driver now held a forty-nine-second lead. George Bignotti grinned wildly and patted Parnelli Jones on the back. Further down the pit area, Foyt's crewmen stood looking out toward the track with drawn faces, perhaps wondering what A. J. would have to say after the race.

A dozen laps behind the leaders, Roger McCluskey rolled on, determined to finish, even if in another man's car. In eight starts at the Speedway, McCluskey had never been running at the end. The vibration bothered him, but not as much as it had Mel Kenyon. He pitted on what was his 158th lap to take fuel.

Two laps later (on what actually was leader Al Unser's 172nd lap) Dan Gurney saw a chunk from the waste gate pipe fly off the car ahead of him going into Turn Three. Gurney missed the pipe, but it hit against the outside wall and bounced down to rest on the white line. The observer on that corner began to reach for the yellow light button.

In that instant, Roger McCluskey ran right over the pipe. The effect was as though some giant had taken a can opener and ripped it along the bottom of his car. His oil tank ruptured. The oil splattered the track under his wheels. McCluskey spun wildly through the turn and banged backward into the outside wall of the chute. The force of the impact ruptured one of the car's full fuel tanks. He would not finish this year either.

* * *

Ronnie Bucknum, coming up fast from behind, braked, spun, and hit the wall. His car began to slide backward across the track. Sammy Sessions saw the wreckage, braked in time to hold some control of his car, then moved high between McCluskey's wreck and the wall. He brushed the wall but kept on going.

Fuel poured in a stream from the side of McCluskey's ruptured tank and now ignited from the hot engine. Brabham spun through the flames, stopped, then continued to the pits. Jerry Grant spun into the infield, killing his engine. McCluskey clambered out of his car. So did Bucknum.

Down the straightaway came Al Unser. He saw the yellow light and braked. His rear end slipped as he passed the wrecked cars, but he did not halt.

Firemen ran to extinguish the blaze. Track guards began directing the race cars through the infield grass to avoid the flames and wreckage. It proved to be an unlucky break for A. J. Foyt. When he downshifted to slow down, the clutch popped on his car. He suddenly discovered he had to hold the gearshift lever to remain running in high gear. An opposite stroke of luck hit Mario Andretti. Mario felt something pop in the rear of his car. All of a sudden, it began to handle properly again. Apparently, a frozen rear axle joint had been causing his trouble. The bumping in the grass loosened it. In the latter stages of the race Mario was able to run his fastest lap of the day: 166.236 mph on lap 193.

McCluskey had earned sixteenth place for Mel Kenyon. Ronnie Bucknum, who injured his knee slightly, was fifteenth. Jerry Grant, meanwhile, received a push to restart his engine. Several laps after the wreck, Jack Brabham's engine blew. He placed thirteenth, ahead of Dick Simon. Simon earlier had spent nearly a half hour in the pits replacing a turbocharger but was still running at the finish. He went 169 laps. The two other back row drivers also finished: Sammy Sessions in twelfth and Jimmy McElreath, who would get fifth.

Bobby Unser dropped out at 192 laps with mechanical trouble. Some people suspected that it had been a part from his car that had triggered the accident. Mel Kenyon knew the identity of the person but refused to point the finger of blame. "It's immaterial," he said. He knew that fate often decided who crashed and who won.

And at that moment, only fate stood between Al Unser and a sweeping victory. Discounting lead changes caused by fuel stops, Unser had stayed in front from the back straightaway of the first lap. But in three of the four previous years, mechanical failure had halted the leader within laps from the finish. It had happened to Al's boss Parnelli Jones in 1967 and to his teammate Joe Leonard in 1968. Would it happen again?

Mark Donohue passed Al Unser, the first car to do so during the race. Foyt passed Unser. But they were still nearly a lap behind. Then Foyt began to lose speed because of his damaged clutch. He no longer could hold his car in high gear. He would spend the last few laps of the race crawling slowly along the inside of the track. It would drop him all the way to tenth place.

For a moment hope reigned in the Penske pits as Mark Donohue cut Unser's lead to forty-six, forty-five, and forty-two seconds. Parnelli Jones ran to the side of the track and waved for Al to go faster. He feared another yellow flag might allow Donohue to close the gap, maybe to win.

Behind the pit wall, however, an official calmly carried the Borg Warner trophy to the winner's circle. It would go to the driver of the Johnny Lightning Special.

The checkered flag flashed for Al Unser.

* * *

Donohue placed second. Then came Gurney. Donnie Allison, who had attracted little attention during the race, crossed the line in fourth. He was named Rookie of the Year. McElreath followed Allison. Those five were the only drivers to complete all 200 laps. As is the custom, Pat Vidan halted the rest of the field in the order in which they were running. Mario Andretti completed 199 laps and Jerry Grant 198.

Rick Muther and Carl Williams went 197 laps. Muther earned his eighth place despite having a fast lap of only 160.994 mph. Williams took ninth despite having driven most of the race minus his fourth gear.

It seemed a sad ending for Team McLaren, which thirty days earlier in May, with three bright orange cars on the track, had seemed unbeatable. There soon would be an even sadder ending. Two days later, Bruce McLaren rammed into an earth bank while testing one of his cars at Goodwood, England. His car exploded. Bystanders dragged McLaren clear of the wreck, but he died within minutes.

* * *

In Victory Lane at Indianapolis on May 30, however, it was a happy moment for Al Unser. He grinned boyishly as he climbed from his car and accepted the applause of 300,000 fans. Cameras clicked and whirred, and Al answered politely the questions thrust at him by the reporters whose stories tomorrow would be read by millions of people all over the world. George Bignotti beamed. So did Al's mother; his wife, Wanda; his brother Bobby; and all of the Johnny Lightning crew in their blue shirts and striped bell-bottom pants. Co-owner Vel Miletich smiled too, and in a great display of self-control, Parnelli Jones didn't kiss his driver.

Back in Gasoline Alley, thirty-two drivers could look forward only to next year. In eleven months, the thirty days of May would begin again. Mario Andretti sat atop a workbench in the STP garage, sipping a soft drink and marveling over how beautifully his car had handled the last few dozen laps. Mark Donohue stood in his garage still dressed in his driving uniform and shook off offers of congratulations: "The only way you can be satisfied is to win," he said.

And A. J. Foyt said more by his actions than by word. He climbed onto his motorcycle and, with his wife, Lucy, riding on the back, grimly drove away.

1970 Indy 500 Race Results

Official Finish		Car Number	Laps Completed
1st:	Al Unser	2	200
2nd:	Mark Donohue	66	200
3rd:	Dan Gurney	48	200
4th:	Donnie Allison	83	200
5th:	Jim McElreath	14	200
6th:	Mario Andretti	1	199
7th:	Jerry Grant	89	198
8th:	Rick Muther	38	197
9th:	Carl Williams	75	197
10th:	A. J. Foyt	7	195
11th:	Bobby Unser	3	192
12th:	Sammy Sessions	67	190
13th:	Jack Brabham	32	175
14th:	Dick Simon	44	168
15th:	Ronnie Bucknum	19	162
16th:	Kenyon/McCluskey	23	160
17th:	Wally Dallenbach	22	143
18th:	Johnny Rutherford	18	135
19th:	Lee Roy Yarbrough	27	107
20th:	George Snider	84	105
21st:	Mike Mosley	9	96
22nd:	Peter Revson	73	87
23rd:	Bill Vukovich	58	78
24th:	Joe Leonard	15	73
25th:	Roger McCluskey	11	62
26th:	Gary Bettenhausen	16	55
27th:	Lloyd Ruby	25	54
28th:	Gordon Johncock	5	45
29th:	Bruce Walkup	97	44
30th:	Art Pollard	10	28
31st:	George Follmer	20	18
32nd:	Greg Weld	93	12
33rd:	Jim Malloy	31	Failed to start

About Retro Reads

Thirty Days in May is part of a series from Octane Press called *Retro Reads*, which reissues high-quality narrative titles and introduces them to a new audience. The series has included several books by Hal Higdon. With *Retro Reads*, motorsports enthusiasts will delight in familiar classics and discover new, dynamic narratives about legendary drivers. Check them out at OctanePress.com, and sign up for our newsletter to learn about all our gearhead-related books.

Made in the USA
Columbia, SC
17 May 2022

60492322R00093